The
Self-Sabotage
Cycle

The
Self-Sabotage
Cycle

Why We Repeat Behaviors that Create
Hardships and Ruin Relationships

Stanley Rosner

Patricia Hermes

Westport, Connecticut
London

Library of Congress Cataloging-in-Publication Data

Rosner, Stanley, 1928–
    The self-sabotage cycle : why we repeat behaviors that create hardships
    and ruin relationships / Stanley Rosner and Patricia Hermes.
       p.   cm.
    Includes bibliographical references and index.
    ISBN 0–275–99003–6 (alk. paper)
    1. Self-defeating behavior.   2. Compulsive behavior.   3. Interpersonal
relations.   I. Hermes, Patricia.   II. Title.
    [DNLM: 1. Compulsive Behavior—psychology.   2. Self-Injurious Behavior.
3. Interpersonal Relations. WM 176 R822s 2006]
  RC455.4.S43S45   2006
  616.85′84–dc22   2006021400

British Library Cataloguing in Publication Data is available

Library of Congress Catalog Card Number: 2006021400
ISBN: 0–275–99003–6

First published in 2006

Praeger Publishers, 88 Post Road West, Westport, CT 06881
An imprint of Greenwood Publishing Group, Inc.
www.praeger.com

Printed in the United States of America

The paper used in this book complies with the
Permanent Paper Standard issued by the National
Information Standards Organization (Z39.48–1984).

10 9 8 7 6 5 4 3 2 1

For Paul Joseph Hermes
P.H.

For My Patients
S.R.

"In Hades he [Sisyphus] was punished by having to try forever to roll a rock uphill which forever rolled back upon him."

Hamilton, E. (1940, 1942). *Mythology. Timeless tales of gods and heroes*. A Mentor Book from New American Library. New York & Scarborough, Ontario

"There's a victory and defeat—the first and best of victories, the lowest and worst of defeats—which each man gains or sustains at the hands not of another, but of himself."

Plato, *Protagoras*

Contents

Acknowledgments

The years of study, of courses, of supervision, and of my personal analysis have served as the foundation for over forty-five years of practice of psychotherapy and psychoanalysis. But this book could not have been written without the teachings of my patients. It was only through them, their efforts to open up their thoughts, memories, and feelings, and their ability to relate to me in their own unique ways that this book could be written. Dynamic psychotherapy and psychoanalysis is an art as well as a science, and its essence lies in the relationship. Part of that relationship consists of my ability to tune in to and to resonate with my patients much like the give and take in playing duets. I know that I have missed cues and that at times there have been dissonances. As in musical composition, where grounding in theory is helpful though it does not make for great music, so also theory in psychoanalytic therapy is necessary though it does not make for successful treatment. It is at least as much a matter of improvisation, intuition, sensitivity, and interpretation. I know that I have not always resonated and that my interpretations have not always been on the mark in the process of playing my part in the many duets, and for that I must live with regrets. My apologia lies in the fact that I have always tried to be attuned and to admit to myself and to my patients when there have been lapses. To the best of my abilities, I have been there for my patients with deep concern and understanding for them. To them, I express my gratitude.

Introduction

It is a late February afternoon and I am standing outside a hotel in Toronto, waiting for a cab to take me to the airport. I have just attended a conference of the American Psychological Association, and as a psychotherapist in private practice, my mind is happily engaged mulling over ideas that have been introduced, new interpretations of what makes man such a wonderfully complex and interesting species. But in spite of, or perhaps because of, my professional preoccupation, I cannot help but notice the hotel doorman. A cheerful type, he opens and closes the hotel door for patrons; opens and closes the doors, smiling and speaking a word to each who comes and goes. I watch him doing this repetitive chore, and wonder how he manages to stay so cheerful. When he has a break for a moment, he comes and chats with me by the curb. As he succeeds in hailing a cab for me, he confides in me. "I wonder how these cabbies do it," he says. "Same thing, day after day, same thing: Drive to the airport and back, the airport and back. It would send me round the bend."

We smile at one another, a hint of camaraderie, of agreement. But I am thinking something. I am thinking how often it is in the nature of man to notice behavior in others that he does not notice in himself—or so it seems to me in my work with patients. And, I see it most often when it comes to this very thing—repetitive behaviors. What is so easily seen in others is so easily hidden from ourselves. Why is this?

Many reasons I suppose. Maybe because our own repetitive behaviors are so imbedded, so instinctual even, that it is impossible to view them on our own. The doorman whose day revolves about opening and closing the door sees no contradiction when he bemoans the fate of the cab driver who must drive to the airport and back day after day after day—because he doesn't see his own behavior as repetitive.

Of course, that is a simple example, a surface contradiction perhaps, and maybe even a self-protective one. Why admit that what I do every hour of every day is unbearably, impossibly repetitive? Maybe by denying it, the individual is better able to perform his job each day. Or perhaps even the doorman's nature is such that all these unique individuals that he comes into contact with are enough stimulation, enough of a change that he does not even feel it as repetitive. Or then again, perhaps he does. How does one know? And does it matter?

In the day-to-day small minutiae of life, no, it does not matter. Many of us do the same things day after day, not just our jobs or professions, our livelihoods, but the most mundane things. Perhaps we like a three-minute egg each morning—not two minutes, not four minutes—three minutes. Or perhaps we might choose, day after day, year after year, to skip breakfast completely.

Some of our repetitious styles are clearly irrational. I had a patient once, a man who always put his left shoe on first—so compulsively, that if by mistake he put on the right shoe first, he'd stop, take it off, and start over again with the left shoe. I know a woman who will stumble across a room in the dark to reach a lamp—because she will not, cannot, turn on an overhead light. So what? The shoe man might end up a bit late for work. The woman might stub her toe. What does it matter?

It matters not at all, unless perhaps these behaviors are symptoms of deeper problems. No, those repetitions, even those compulsions, are not what draw me to contemplate this matter of repetition. What draws me is the extent to which I see other kinds of repetitive behaviors in my practice—repetitions that ruin lives, repetitions that drive individuals almost to madness, repetitions that can even lead to suicide. Yet many, if not most, of these self-defeating, destructive repetitive behaviors are almost totally out of the conscious realm. That is what tugs at me most.

Shortly after I began debating these issues with myself, I was asked to consult with a man who seemed to have everything going for him. Louis was fortyish, a successful businessman who appeared to be happily married, the father of a "great kid," as he called his son of ten, doing well in his career and personal life. But he came to me because he was restless and wondered about the meaning of life. And, as he revealed after a few sessions, he was involved with another woman—one whom, he admitted, he did not love. Yet even without love, Louis was on the verge of leaving his family. He did not understand his own behavior and had sufficient insight to know that something was wrong. Not only that, he had vowed that he would never do to his family what his own father had done to him. What developed over the course of the next many sessions came as something of a shock—not necessarily to me, but clearly to Louis. In talking, he revealed that his own father had left the family when Louis was about the same age as Louis's son was now—ten years old. In addition, Louis's father's father, his grandfather, had also left his family when his son was ten. Louis was about to become the third father in the family to abandon his wife and children. Louis had known these things somewhere in his head, because he brought the issues up to me. But he had never made the connection. It was only when I pointed out the ages of the boys who were abandoned by their fathers—ten years old, the same age as Louis's son—that he said, "You mean I'm doing the same thing?"

I chose not to reply because sometimes silence is the most powerful response. But Louis didn't need my response. Tears welled in his eyes and for a moment he had to stop to collect himself. Yet it was the opening we had both been looking for—the time when Louis could see what was happening—and more to the point perhaps—why it was happening. For Louis, looking at the cycle of repetition was the first step in gaining some mastery over what he was causing to happen unconsciously.

Perhaps, one might think, Louis is an exception. Surely, there are few individuals constantly repeating behaviors that are self-destructive. One might sensibly ask if I am not exaggerating. After all, if humans are motivated by pleasure, as Freud has suggested, then surely good sex, good food, fun, and comfort all would seem to call to us. So it may very well seem implausible to believe that an individual

---

would keep on doing the very things that hurt. I agree that it may seem that way. However, my experience suggests that it is plausible and it is possible. And it happens all of the time. One need not be in my profession to see how this spins out in daily life. Simply read the newspapers, turn on the television, read history books. Examples abound of a repetition of truly self-destructive themes alive and well in many of us.

Take the successful businessman who repeatedly risks reputation and money on high stakes, and even illegal bets, until eventually he is found out. And loses everything. Or many of us have known—or known of—a man who marries for the second and third and even fourth time, marrying the same type of woman who didn't please or satisfy him the first time around. We, his neighbors and friends, perhaps, might see that the new wife is much the same as the earlier versions of herself in his life—but he marries her nevertheless. He is unaware of this repetition, until she too no longer pleases him. Consider the woman who grew up with a tyrant for a father, a man who was physically and perhaps even sexually abusive—and yet she marries the same kind of man and ends up often in a hospital emergency room. Yet that woman doesn't see any connection between her abusive father and her abusive husband.

Consider the child whose mother committed suicide in her middle years when her child was still very young—and when that child is grown and in her own middle years, she too takes her own life. Is suicide contagious? Or is this too, a form of deep-seated, unrecognized repetition—do unto others as has been done unto me?

What is important to recognize here is that such lives are bedeviled and destroyed by these compulsions to repeat these unrecognized compulsions. When I say "compulsion" here, I am not referring only to the classic repetition compulsion that Freud wrote about. To Freud, who was the first to define it, the classical repetition compulsion was so instinctual as to be next to impossible to bring to the surface, nearly impossible to face head-on and change. What I refer to here is a less instinctual, but just as insidious, type of repetition, the unconscious need to repeat something again and again, a drive to carry out an act regardless of the consequences, even if it destroys one's life and happiness.

I'm thinking of an attractive young woman, Cory, who came to me with a very practical concern. She wanted help prioritizing her time, her tasks. She wanted help in organizing her work life. It seemed an oddly limited request for such a bright, capable young woman. Cory had graduated from a fine college and fine law school and had gotten a job, over fierce competition, with a large, high-powered law firm. But after a while there, she had run into difficulties meeting schedules, prioritizing her time, and eventually she had been told that she was not on track for a partnership with the firm. And so, she had left. Now, she was starting her own law firm, but was facing difficulties here, too, forgetting things, creating scheduling conflicts. When I tried to probe deeper into her background, she became impatient with me. "I want to focus on the problem at hand," she replied. "Time management. I'm not concerned with long ago."

Although I did not yet say so, I had a thought that I have so often with patients early on in their therapy—*You act as though you were born yesterday, as though you just appeared here, hatched out of an egg.* But Cory did eventually talk about her earlier life. And it soon became clear that for Cory, it was a profound piece of miscasting that had her living out this life as a high-powered attorney. And unconsciously or not, she was sabotaging herself. Her father had chosen her as the one he wanted to "succeed," indeed, as the son he had never had. All of his focus was on seeing Cory as successful in a "man's world." And while that might not have been bad were it Cory's wish for herself, in fact, it was not. She had other goals for herself, some of which she had never even identified until much later in our work together.

Why? Because the early conflicts had not been resolved. Cory and her internalized father figure were pushing and pulling at one another, in dismal repetition of what had gone on in her earlier life. But she didn't know this, at least not on the surface, and so, was doomed to repeat it.

Is there a point at which one is able to recognize such repetitions? Can anyone come to this realization? And can the cycle really change?

Hard questions. But I do believe that the answers are yes. And sometimes. Though I admit it's not easy. Individuals who have spent a lifetime building their view of themselves and their world around a certain perception—or misperception—can be afraid to challenge that view, and understandably so.

Essie came to me for the first time on September 11, 2001. Now many of us, in fact probably all of us, were traumatized in some way by the events of that stupendously horrible day. Certainly those who were there, who were injured, who lost loved ones, were most traumatically involved. But Essie had not been at Ground Zero. She had not known anyone who had been. But from the moment the World Trade Center collapsed in ashes, her world turned to ashes around her. She felt traumatized, terrified. Worst of all, she was almost totally unable to function. Even the drive to my office was an almost insurmountable task for her.

But she came. With time and talking, it became clear that Essie had come to me with a very clear view of herself as one who was frightened, unable to hold onto the world as an adult, one who complained and hung back, terrified of the most ordinary daily events. This was her mode of operation long before that day. But now, with these awful events, she was plunged into near despair.

Certain insights followed in the many months that we worked together. One was particularly poignant when Essie was able to confront an event that she had known dimly but refused to acknowledge for a very long time: Her father had been having sex with her from the time she was nine years old until she was fourteen, when she was old enough to forcefully insist that he stop. She had never told her mother about the incest, feeling that she would not be believed. As she was finally able to tell me this, her eyes filled with tears. She actually looked pale. I almost felt that I was holding my breath, wondering how she would deal with this fact, the fact that her entire life, all her feelings of helplessness and fear and even despair, had been based on this fact: that she felt she had no choice but to submit, no ability to fight, no right to speak up for herself. All of her inner and outer life had been based on this awful event, this feeling of having no control, that had shaped her life. I also knew at this point things that Essie had yet to realize—that she had been cheated out of childhood by her father, her adult sexual life destroyed by him, and perhaps by her mother's silent complicity. No wonder the events of 9/11 brought her to that point of panic and despair. It was the sense of total helplessness that swept up so many of us on that awful day that reawakened her own horrible feelings of being the child who had no say. The recognition was a somber, bitter moment. It was somber for both of us.

What happened with Essie, the burying of traumatic feelings, experiences, and memories, happens with many people. However, burying these experiences does not mean that they are dead. Rather, they become incorporated, become an indelible part of the image that individuals have of themselves. Essie was the helpless child who felt fragile, exposed to a dangerous world. She carried this image into adulthood in the way she viewed herself and the way she related to others. She didn't know why and she couldn't account for this. There was a gap between how she felt about herself and the basis for such feelings. In many ways, children don't have control over their lives and Essie was stuck in this child's place.

Surprising as it may seem, it can be hard for me, too, to be part of this exhuming of buried painful emotions and memories. How can I justify pulling out material from the unconscious, material that the patient has sometimes worked an entire life at concealing, not only from the outside world, but from him or herself? If it was hidden, there was undoubtedly a good reason for hiding it. Do I dare to dig at it, poke at it, perhaps cause pain by bringing it to consciousness? After all, the past cannot change, so what is the point of it all? The point is to bring it to consciousness. But it is also much more than that. The child inside the adult, the child who buried the traumatic past, relives it again and again in an unconscious attempt to gain mastery over those uncontrollable events. The point therefore, is to enable change, to enable the helpless child to become the adult who is no longer stuck, feeling that she has no control over her life. With awareness and memory, these events can be viewed differently.

And change and awareness are inextricably intertwined. But therein lies the art and science of psychotherapy—and yes, it is an art. I must be sure that the relationship between me and the patient is trustworthy and solid enough to explore this material. Timing is everything. A principle task of psychoanalysis is to make what is unconscious, conscious. But it is not a task that can be undertaken unless there is that solid connection. It hurts the patient, and sometimes even the therapist. Isn't it better left alone? Some individuals might say yes. And some have said yes—and walked away from therapy. That is their right. It is not for me to judge that one ought or ought not have therapy. But if the individual has come to me hoping for change, if the issue that brought her there is difficult enough—as it was for Essie—then maybe it is worth the pain and the fear and the turmoil, the bitter sense that a good portion of life has been wasted. Because it is only by bringing it into consciousness that other things can change. Secrets hidden cause symptoms, as with Essie. I can, and often do, tell a patient that "late" is better than "never." But we both know that it is still bitter. As for myself, it gives me no pleasure to see patients suffer pain, to be reduced to tears, to expose what they have spent a lifetime keeping repressed. But sometimes such suffering must come before the problems can be resolved, and helping to work through those problems is my job.

While exposing vulnerabilities and facing unpleasant things that have long been buried is a necessary first part, it is sometimes the easy part. What comes next is the hard part—translating that recognition into a change in behavior—because change is not an intellectual exercise. Unless that recognition is internalized, is felt, is acted upon, nothing will change. Can recalling experiences, feelings, and memories of the past, some of which have been repressed, some which have been only vaguely remembered, actually lead to change, to a new way of seeing one's self and the world? Can this be the beginning of a new perception of one's self, free of the distortions and the unexplained symptoms that persisted since childhood? How can I best facilitate the process of change?

For this too is true: Analysts are human beings; analysts have feelings, too. Although I have at times referred to myself as a dinosaur, one who follows a more traditional kind of therapeutic mode than many today, I am not a mere spectator in this process. The notion of the uninvolved analyst who falls asleep in session or who simply mutters, "Hmm," and "Ah," are mostly fictions of old movies and bad TV shows. Yes, there was a time when the analyst was much more removed from his or her patient, and even today, in certain types of analysis, some of that distance is maintained. But today, there are as many types of therapy as there are therapists, and most of them are much more involved with the patient. For myself, I prefer what Freud has called maintaining "evenly hovering attention." That, however, does not mean uninvolved attention. On the contrary, it means attuned attention, awareness of my own reactions to what is being communicated as well as the way in which it is being communicated. It means reflecting back to the patient what I think is really meant. Often I remark, following something that has been said, "What did you say?" I say that, not because I didn't hear the remark, but to encourage the patient to hear himself and to hear the implications of the remark. Free expression of thoughts and feelings, what we call free association, can superficially sound like a series of unrelated meanderings. However, these thoughts are anything but. It is my task to underline and to articulate the connections, to establish new insights, to resonate with feelings and moods.

And so yes, I feel compassion. And sadness. And fear. I occasionally feel the joy of discovery, of two individuals being on the same path to renewal, two who share an experience that is life-changing. I care. I feel. Intensely.

But I can also feel annoyed, bored, restless. At one time I had as a patient, Betty, a woman who was living with a husband who was abusive, both mentally and occasionally physically. Week after week, Betty began her session saying, "You won't believe what he did this week!" Week after week, I listened; week after week, she said she'd had enough. Week after week, we agreed she'd be better off if she left him. And *week* after *week*, after *week* Betty returned to him—and returned to me—with the same refrain: *You won't believe what he did this week*. After a while, I found that not only was Betty saying the same thing, I was saying the same thing. And I began to feel for a while that I was the one who was being repetitive. I sometimes wanted to shake her, to shout: *Why are you staying when you have said a thousand times that you will leave him? Can't you see what you are doing?* But that is not how therapy works. Sometimes even, in my own dark nights of the soul, I wonder if therapy can work at all in cases such as Betty's. But we both persevere. Because Betty is, in important ways, a child, a child who feels that all she has is that abusive parent. She feels there is no other choice but to remain with that abusing parent, because the alternative is total abandonment, even annihilation.

So, if repetitions abound, and we struggle to understand and to quell them, it's reasonable to ask—why? Is there a compulsion to repeat, an *instinct* to repeat such behavior as was suggested by Freud?[1] And if so, why the self-destructive repetitions? How do we explain, not only repetition of self-destructive *acts*, but the repetition of painful experiences in dreams and memories? Are such things attempts at mastery, attempts to change the outcome *just for once?* Or does the repetition itself, even if painful, offer some peculiar gain? Freud thought he had this figured out through his work with traumatized World War I veterans. He found that these men endlessly reenacted and dreamed of their terrible war experiences, leading him to the notion of thanatos, the instinct toward death. It was a controversial idea in his time, and has remained so. And yet—and yet—I believe that though the idea of the death instinct may well be questionable, the compulsion to repeat self-destructive actions and thoughts is not at all in dispute.

But even accepting that this is so, I return to the question that is much more to the point: Is such behavior subject to change? Is there hope for those who suffer acutely, if unconsciously, from such repetitive behavior? Is there hope for Betty and Cory and Louis and all the many others who have come to me over the years, bedeviled by unconscious repetitive behaviors? Can change occur? Is there hope for change? I think so. And that is where my work comes in, and what this book is all about. It is an attempt to show just how these repetitive behaviors can be exposed, brought into light, and yes, even changed.

Yes? But how?

Anna O, a patient of Freud's, coined the phrase, the "talking cure." Freud's "talking cure," if we can call it that, has had an undeniable affect on our culture, on our beliefs, even on our vocabulary. All, or almost all, of modern psychotherapies, owe a great deal to Freudian underpinnings.

When I meet a new patient, I invariably feel a kind of tension. Can I help achieve some kind of healing? Can we build a relationship; can we find a plane of communication? Or will this intercourse be doomed to failure? It is never clear at the beginning. And though one can very occasionally say with some certainty that this or that is the *goal*, even the goal is hardly ever clear in the beginning. Some people have preconceived notions of what therapy is. They want answers. They want advice. They sometimes want, as did Cory, to act as though they were born yesterday—and that long-ago feelings and traumas have no bearing on their problems of today.

Certainly, there are forms of therapy that do not involve delving into the past. Indications, based on empirical evidence, are that some of these forms of therapy are clearly effective. Such therapies may deal only with the here and now and are aimed simply at giving patients an opportunity to express their feelings. Patients can change because they see the self-defeating results of their behavior. Such therapies can help alleviate fears and resolve problems with relationships, relieve anxieties and depression. There may even be a ripple effect where changes in overt behavior filter down to the unconscious, enabling some deeper problems to get resolved. However, it is extremely unlikely that any of these forms of therapy are successful in dealing with the kinds of self-destructive, repetitive behavior that we talk about here.

Resolution of these deeper, unconscious forms of repetition demand delving into the past. They demand opening up the roots of unconscious conflicts, understanding the underlying reasons for behavior, making what is unconscious conscious, enabling the individual to perceive himself and the world around him differently. That is the ultimate goal and resolution—providing individuals with freedom to choose what they want. A basic tenet is that behavior is motivated by dynamic factors which often elude awareness. Our goal is to bring those factors into awareness in order to facilitate personality change. Behavioral change follows personality change. It is only there that repetitive cycles of self-sabotage can be resolved.

The practice of dynamic psychotherapy is exciting and awe-inspiring. Regardless of the number of patients seen and the thousands of hours spent practicing psychotherapy, I am in awe of humankind's capacity to find ways to protect and defend a sense of integrity. The need to survive, to test limits, to find excuses and rationalizations in order to feel a sense of control are as varied as are people. No two are alike when it comes to psychological makeup. Each brings a unique history. Each has a story to tell. Each has unique defenses. Patients may be poverty-ridden or wealthy, physically strong or feeble, bright or of mediocre intelligence. They may have different cultural and ethnic backgrounds and vastly different temperaments. Inheritance may set important limits on the way they view and deal with the various trials and tribulations of life. Temperament can determine reactions to life, but biology is not to be dismissed, either. Even some forms of mental illness are determined by genetics. But beyond the constraints imposed by any one of these things, we are all significantly affected by our individual nurture and history and environment. No two people experience the same environment, and the world is ever changing, environments are ever-changing. Heraclitus said that one never steps into the same stream twice.

While there are labels, diagnoses, categories, no single person fits neatly into any one. But all people are, in the end, similar, for we all are human, human and unique. Each problem is unique. Each way of dealing with the past is unique. It is humbling to appreciate the wide range of variations as individuals deal with successes and failures, with victories and disappointments, with threats and fears. The differences far outweigh the similarities, and each new patient presents a unique challenge.

It is a difficult terrain that we embark on. Mostly, I find myself wondering if we can sort out the ordinary human miseries, the ones that bedevil all of us humans, from the other kinds of miseries, the evil, noxious ones that reside in the recesses of injured souls. I often tell patients I have nothing to offer them but change. But that is not quite true. What I have to offer is the *opportunity* for change.

It happens sometimes in the course of therapy that such an opportunity never arises. Sometimes it is because the patient is unable or unwilling to change or even to bring up the material or gain access to the feelings that could help that change. Sometimes it is because individuals are afraid. They come to me because on the surface they want change, but there is another part of them that fears change. And it is that second part that wins in the struggle.

But just as often, I must ask myself this: Where am I failing this patient? What am I missing? Is my silence too much? Or, conversely, am I talking too much? Surely, in any session, hints are being thrown out, messages are given, sometimes just by the patient's physical appearance. Is she slovenly looking today? Are his shoulders slumped? Is she unusually lively? Is he ready—ready to make that leap? For it is surely a leap of faith that leads one to truly begin this very, very scary journey. Yes, coming to a therapist's office is a beginning, but it is only a beginning. It can take many, many months—years even—before a true relationship evolves. And it is in the relationship that change takes place.

For me, I find that my psychotherapy must be almost constantly reinvented. For all the literature about the science of psychotherapy, it is, after all, a subjective and creative art. And just as it is unlikely that we can find unanimous agreement about what constitutes good art, so it is unlikely to find unanimity of agreement as to what constitutes good therapy. For each person, it is a different journey. For each person, I am different. As one of my mentors put it, we are each, patient and therapist, embarking on a trip through an unknown jungle. Neither of us has ever been in this particular jungle before. The only difference between me and the patient is that I have been through other jungles before—not this particular one, but others. I have a bit of a feel for how to negotiate the various paths and traps of the jungle.

Not only is the patient different each time, but even I am a different person each time an individual patient encounters me. I am mother. I am father. I am envious or envied sibling. I am teacher. I am the molester or even abuser. I am anyone but me. I must allow patients to make of me who they will, but at the same time remain myself for each of them. I must be finely attuned to my own feelings, memories, and thoughts. I must trust my feelings and thoughts because they are important clues as to what is happening in the interchange between us. It's a scary journey. It is not for cowards, whether patient or therapist. But it is, perhaps, the most rewarding kind of journey. It can even be music.

Is it for everyone? No. But I truly believe it is the only way to halt the cycle of repetition. And—*it takes time*. In this day of managed care, in our rush to get everything done now and quickly, there is little patience with the kind of talking therapy that takes the one thing we have so little of—time. Who wants to spend months, years even, to achieve change? Not only that, but with the proliferation of drugs to soothe and lift every mood and depression and disorder, why talk? Approximately one in ten Americans are or have been taking one of the mood enhancing drugs on the market today. Drugs may offer relief from anxiety but they do nothing to help in dealing with the compulsion to repeat.

There is another more insidious reason, I believe, that works against this talking cure: Though many, many people, especially in the arts and theatre, have talked openly about their therapy, it is still very much of a taboo in our society. Even with the proliferation of movies and TV shows and books about therapy, the common view is that therapy is either for rich neurotics or for those who are truly unstable. In addition, the movies and TV shows that portray therapists as bumblers or evil-doers do nothing to encourage public confidence. Why, any normal person might wonder, would I subject myself to such wicked ministrations? And *pay* for it, to boot? Also, perhaps surprisingly, the shows that portray the therapist as heroic can be just as bad, making a patient long for a therapeutic relationship that has been conceived in a fantasy land, building up expectations that are doomed from the start.

There is another reason that the "talking cure" is not used commonly, and it is this: What happens when the world at large finds out that one has been or is in therapy? In the field of politics, that can be a death blow. A politician today can be revealed to have had extra-marital affairs, can admit to drug use, can even be convicted of drunken driving and survive these things. Many have. But rare is the politician who can survive the revelation of psychotherapeutic intervention. Such an admission has done in more than one politician in recent history.

So yes, there are many reasons for individuals choosing not to engage in this difficult task. And besides, there is always this question in the back of one's mind: Can *talking* really *cure,* especially the kind of talking done in the psycho-analytic mode? Will it really make a difference in my life?

It is a question I am asked often. In fact, it is a question I asked myself when I first went into training as a psychoanalytic therapist. To be qualified, I had to undergo psychoanalysis myself. I remember asking my mentor why I needed to do this. I had had some therapy before, and felt no need of more.

"Oh?" he said. "So you want to analyze but you don't want to *be* analyzed?"

Well, no. It's uncomfortable. It's unsettling. It's—scary!

It is. For all of us. It often reveals things that we would rather keep hidden, even from ourselves. It may, perhaps, show us as merely human when we would like to think of ourselves as noble or saintly, or at least free of problems and foibles. It may show that we have weakness and defects, and that we are not immune to the defects that we see in others. For me, it was uncomfortable, yes. Very. But it also revealed to me some valuable lessons in humility and wonder and awe, lessons that I would badly need in my work with patients— the humility of knowing that no person is really totally knowable; the wonder, even the awe of realizing that a human being would so generously open his or her soul to me. And the knowledge that I had better be careful with it.

So yes, I believe in talking. I believe in the building of the therapeutic relationship so that change can occur. There are many theories about how and why this happens. That can be left for later. For now though, I believe it is through case histories that I can best *show* what happens in the talking cure, show how change can come about as two very fallible human beings traverse some very difficult terrain. With hard work on the part of both patient and therapist. With caring. With time. And with just a little bit of luck.

Chapter 1

Repetition of Early Identifications: Conformity vs. Autonomy

Many of us love to create, to experiment, to travel, to learn, to grow—to *become*. But there are others among us who are not only unable to face such challenges and adventures, but are literally unable to even imagine such a thing. Such individuals cling to the belief that the only way, the only really good and right way, to lead one's life is to follow precisely in the footsteps of others, and most often that "other" is the parent. Such aping of the parent in an almost identical way is referred to as "archaic identification." The little girl who clomped around in her mother's high-heeled shoes grows up to be an adult who must wear the same style shoes. The young boy whose family vacationed at a cabin on Rainbow Lake year after year grows up and insists on taking his own family to the same cabin on Rainbow Lake—sometimes, much to the dismay of his current family. Others cook the same way their mothers cooked (even if the results could stand improvement), go to the same churches, synagogues, and mosques, attend the same theatres, and sometimes even live in the same houses. For these individuals, in their real lives, and in their inner lives, there is no room for change, for innovation, no room even for imagination.

So what is it that makes individuals engage in this repetitive behavior, this archaic identification, even at the cost of self? If one were to ask, most often the response would be: Well, it's the right way. It's also comfortable and it's familiar, and change is not easy. Young children seek and need structure. They need models for their behavior. They look to their parents for leadership. So what's wrong with that?

Nothing, of course. What is wrong though is that some parents communicate to their children the belief that their way *alone* is superior to all others. The child grows up believing that anyone other than the parent is inferior. No one is as good or as right as the parents. In support of their own views, such parents may mock the permissiveness of others or the neatness of others or the lifestyle of others. And this can be true, even when terrible things are happening in the home. If parents are spendthrifts buying everything in sight, the child gets the idea that this is the way things should be. The child is not aware that the parents may be on the verge of bankruptcy. If the parents are alcoholics and the house is a mess, then the child gets the idea that this is the way parents are and this is the way homes are supposed to be. If the parents are harsh and punitive, then the message is that this is the way to maintain discipline and to curb one's dangerous and unruly appetites.

It is only as the child gets older and sees other lifestyles that he or she may begin to question whether the family's style really is the only or the best style. And, though this should be a normal state of development, in repressive families such as I refer to here, it is at this point that terrible struggles can begin, sometimes even lifelong struggles. How can one question such dominating and controlling parents? The child becomes terribly afraid. It is a real fear and an enormous one because it involves the one thing we all need and the one thing for which we all yearn—love. If the unloving family attitude states, *I can't like you unless you're like me*—the child accepts that he is only lovable by being, not himself, but his parents.

And so it is set in motion, the repetitive lifestyle of archaic identification—absolute identification with the parents. This in itself is tragedy enough.

The next tragedy is that the adult child now carries on doing things exactly as the parent did, always reaching for the goal of love—by behaving exactly like the parent. It's a sad way to live a life, and in my experience working with such burdened individuals, it's a difficult way of life to change. The growing child could not risk being herself because it brought rejection and anger. The adult child carries that forward. But there is another underlying struggle now going on. Those who copy their parents excessively deny and cover over their legitimate wishes to be free.

I want so much to be free. I want so very much to be free. And I am so awfully mad at you for not allowing my freedom. But I need you. Without you, I am alone. I know how to fix this. I'll be just like you, just the way you want me to be, and then you'll love me, and neither you nor I will know how much I hate you, how badly I want to be free of you.

Scary, and sad too. Because their way is right and other ways are wrong, those who repeat these early identifications fall into the same pattern. Theirs is the best of all possible worlds; theirs is the right and proper code of behavior.

And so, how do such individuals fare in therapy? And why would such an individual even consider therapy? After all, he or she is doing exactly what is right.

Sometimes such an individual comes into therapy because of conflict caused by outside forces. Perhaps it happens from meeting new people or even falling in love. The loved one may be someone who believes and acts differently from the original family, who questions the standards and values of the family. This can begin to undermine the belief system that has been accepted and adhered to for years. What happens next is great inner turmoil and, with it, great strain on the relationship with the family of origin.

Still though, this can be a good beginning, if quite frightening. Yet here, often the individual becomes stuck. He cannot continue to suppress the urge toward autonomy. Yet he doesn't dare to go forward, and can't go back. What to do? Some move sideways. They find themselves acting passive-aggressively, outwardly agreeing with and buying into the parental strictures while behaving in ways that undermine themselves and the strictures. The resulting conflicts take a toll on the individual and on the relationship with the family.

This can be the time when certain individuals may enter therapy. Sometimes even this happens at the behest of the parents in the expectation that therapy will "straighten" the child out—that is, make the child conform. With treatment, the parent hopes the child will cease the passive-aggressive behavior and be more passively conforming.

I'm thinking of Valerie, an attractive young married woman who worked for long hours and for little compensation in her mother's obsolete business. Her new husband urged her to leave the business and enter the new technological world where, with her background, she could be hugely successful. Valerie couldn't, and there were struggles. In Valerie's mind, it was not her relationship with her mother that prompted her to enter psychotherapy, but conflict in the marriage. In the course of therapy, Valerie expressed anger at her husband who earned a lot more money working fewer hours than she did. She viewed him as spoiled, selfish, and looking for the easy way out. She was filled with righteous indignation feeling that her mother's hard work and her hard work were "holier" than his easy way of life. He was successful, respected in his field, and had spare time besides! As we talked, she became even more irritated with her husband. She also became very irritated with me for questioning her position.

Why was this bright capable woman so tied to the old and the obsolete? Why did she feel so indignant at others, including her husband, who succeeded without struggling? She continually reminded herself—and me—of how difficult a life her mother had. Her father had died in an accident when she was a young child and he had just started the business when he died. She knew—she had been told a thousand, a million times—how her mother struggled and sacrificed to run that same business in order to support and raise Valerie. How could Valerie not feel guilty and obliged? There was a clear message that Valerie had no choice but to help her mother. If she did not conform to her mother's wishes, she would be an ingrate who would not be accepted by her mother. Neither could she accept her resentment at working long hours in a business she disliked for little compensation. But she could not admit this to herself.

Valerie did agree that her mother was a martyr. I reminded her that martyrs are often very angry people. I also said that in my experience there is no stronger glue than guilty rage that binds a child to a parent. The rage is denied and buried while the "good" girl is up on stage, acting her good girl part.

Valerie absorbed this quietly—and slowly. Eventually, she began to pay lip service to understanding. But there was still a long way to go before there would be change—because intellectual understanding is not at all the same as emotional understanding, the kind of understanding that can possibly lead to change. After a few months of sessions, I felt free to wonder aloud how, if Valerie felt this way about her mother, she had even allowed herself to get married. Sheepishly, she admitted that her mother liked her husband and encouraged her relationship with him. Valerie admitted that she couldn't believe that her mother was so agreeable to this relationship when she was so negative toward other men Valerie went out with. Thoughts had crossed Valerie's mind that something seemed strange about this, but she could not understand it. Her mother's approval served to propel the relationship further, leading to marriage, about which even Valerie had doubts. "He was so different and his family seemed so much at ease and so comfortable that I felt I didn't belong."

It was quite by accident that Valerie's mother let slip that since Valerie's future husband came from a more affluent background, he would be able to help her business financially. Her mother gave her stamp of approval to the marriage based upon her own needs. Her own. Not her daughter's. This open recognition of her mother's exploitative behavior, even to the point of approving her husband, not for Valerie's sake, but for *mother's business*, came as a terrific blow to Valerie. Valerie not only saw what was happening—she *felt* it. She absorbed it. She was, in fact, devastated by it.

It was only after this that she began to really comprehend the degree to which her life had been devoted to pleasing her mother at her own expense. And it was only then that things began to change. Eventually, not right away, she was able to disengage from her mother, but not without a fight, not without her mother laying guilt on her and even threatening to disown her. Yet Valerie persisted. She began to look for a new job. Eventually, she did it—broke those ties with her mother, found herself a more gratifying job that paid much more. She continued to help her mother financially, but the strangulating bond was broken.

Valerie had been at risk of not only continuing this harmful connection with her mother but of repeating the same with others—with her husband and with any children she might have in the future. She could easily have become the martyred—and angry—wife and mother, the same as her mother. She could have lived with the guilt that paralyzed; she could have assumed an indignant attitude toward anyone who had an easier life than she and her mother did. (She had been on her way toward that when she began therapy.) Her marriage could easily have dissolved and her future would have been to perpetuate the bond with her mother. The price for separating from the mother was high. It was difficult, and Valerie needed a great deal of support to withstand her own guilt and the constant blame that her mother imposed on her. She could easily have continued working long hours for very little compensation. But she didn't. Instead, she maintained a cordial relationship with her mother, a relationship different and more distant than it had been. Valerie had to go through turmoil to break away. Damage had been done, and now Valerie's job was to try and change—to fix what could be fixed.

When Valerie had first married and moved into a house that was far more luxurious than she ever dreamed of, she had become extremely difficult in the marriage. The kitchen was too small, the bedrooms had to be rearranged, and buying furniture was a nightmare of indecisions, as she ordered and then cancelled orders, then ordered again. Valerie could not allow herself to enjoy this new lifestyle with pleasure. Following the change in her relationship with her mother, there was a ripple effect. Valerie became a more independent, self-motivated person. She no longer suffered the self-doubts and guilt that she had lived with for her whole life. She was able to invest herself in her marriage as well as do well on her new job.

It was a pretty much happy ending.

Mary's story is a different story. Mary was utterly attached to her family of origin and particularly to her mother. Mother believed that family came first. Mother believed that all kinds of sacrifices should be made to maintain the sanctity of family. Mother taught Mary that anything that takes the wife and husband away from one another and especially from the children was bad. But Mother did not marry Carlo. Mary married Carlo. And Carlo, a good man, had different ideas of family. He was a carpenter who worked hard and came home every night to be with his wife and two young children. But Carlo, at the age of thirty, decided he wanted a different kind of life. He had never been much of a student and had squeaked through high school without studying or doing much homework. After four years of marriage and two kids, he wanted to enter the business world. He felt at a disadvantage, never having disciplined himself to study. And so, he wanted to learn and to enroll in school.

Prior to doing this, he discussed his wishes and plans with Mary and she agreed. It would be difficult working all day and going to school at night with other students who were already steeped in study, they both agreed. But he was highly motivated. And so he went. He spent weekends in the library. At home, Mary became more and more angry. While she had paid lip service to his wanting to "better himself" and to follow his dreams, she now saw his absences as rejection of her and the children. She howled that this was not her idea of family life and insisted that she wanted a husband who was home with the family. (Basically, Mary was threatened, fearing that Carlo would become involved with other women who were more geared to careers. She also felt she was going to be left out of his life at college and eventually from the corporate life to which Carlo aspired.) But more than that, she could not move away from what she believed to be the role of a "real family"—that is, a family like Mom's. She refused to support his efforts, and dragged him off to therapy with me.

In the therapy sessions she did not like anything she heard, or perhaps the truer statement is that she did not hear anything. She did not hear my questions. She did not hear my concerns. She, of course, wanted to hear nothing from Carlo. She wanted only to tell me that her complaints were supported by her mother and her siblings. She wanted only to tell me that Carlo's behavior undermined the family's conception of "family." Carlo, she said, was the black sheep of the family and she was fed up.

He, in turn, felt ostracized and undermined. He believed he was trying to support his family financially and emotionally. He was trying to improve his lot in life and that of his family at great cost to himself. But it was all for naught.

It became clear that Mary had always had difficulty with change. Suffering from phobias as a child, she could not tolerate the thought of traveling or vacationing, anything that would take her away from home. The marriage became increasingly alienated, but somehow, limped on, though they did not continue to come to me in therapy.

Five years later though, they did return. Carlo now was working in finance and was enrolled in an MBA program, working very hard, commuting long hours, and earning more money than he had ever dreamed of. Mary viewed him as an elitist. The marriage was in serious trouble. Mary fully expected that this time I was going to tell Carlo that he needed to shape up. (It seemed interesting to me that she should insist on returning to me though we had made almost no progress in our previous attempt. And sad to say, we made none here, either.)

In the chapter on marriage, we discuss the unwritten contract.[1] It might be said that Carlo broke the original contract with Mary. She expected him to be a carpenter who would be happy working and being with his family. No matter that she had agreed with Carlo's plans for self-betterment. No matter that he did not do this unilaterally without discussing it with her. No, there were different things at issue here: Mary had a set of values and ideals set forth by her mother, and though Carlo's values were good, healthy, strong ones, she could not see that. She fought to keep things precisely the same as they had been in her childhood, with devastating results—as the marriage faltered and eventually failed.

I have frequently been asked, when an individual first comes to consult me, if I am a "Christian therapist." The assumption seems to be that I can only help those who share the same myth/belief system as do they. Fred grew up in a religiously fundamentalist home in which the literal words of the Bible, of the pastor, of the tight religious community were law. Fred had to attend religious instruction and prayer early every morning before going off to a religiously affiliated school. Every evening was devoted to study and prayer. There was no fun. There was no socializing. His parents were extremely strict and rigid and demanded total conformity of their oldest son. But there was a problem. Fred was extremely bright and inquisitive. He had questions. There were things he didn't understand. Yet when he asked those questions, he was not just silenced, he was roared at. Questions were the work of the devil!

And so Fred stuffed down his questions, and tried to be the good son. But after a while, he developed tics and speech difficulties. His parents attributed these to his "straying from the word of the Lord."

There was no thought of getting therapy for Fred because his symptoms were caused by his willful, sinful, and rebellious behavior. Fred persisted in his doubts and skepticism, though he did it mostly silently. Still, there was a price to pay, for his parents knew his doubts—and his peers tormented him for his twitching and stammering. When he was accepted by a top-notch college to which he applied secretly, his parents demanded that he go to a college that was affiliated with the religion. Fred fought them. They refused to pay for secular college. He got a scholarship and worked for money for books and personal expenses. He was a straight A student. He distanced himself from his parents. At their urging, he came home on some holidays only to be met with demands that he go to church and behave the way they wanted him to. He returned to school and began drinking and spending much time just playing cards, hanging out at bars, having sex. He was in a state of guilty rebellion. The result was increasing alienation between him and his parents—and between Fred and himself.

Another problem was going on at home, and it wasn't just with Fred. His mother had a fragile hold on reality, and Fred recognized this. When his father was shouting at his mother to pray, Fred sometimes tried to rescue her only to be blamed for being the cause of his parents' arguments. "If you only minded your own business and went to church, we'd all be better off," his father would say. His mother ended up in mental institutions a number of times. Each time she was released, his father said he had saved her through prayer. As Fred grew and separated from his family, he continued to surreptitiously keep in touch with his younger brother who was still acceding to his parents and viewed Fred as a pariah. Fred felt depressed and lonely with no support other than his friends at college who commiserated with him. But that did little to help his feelings of alienation. His parents told him that he was not welcome in the home unless he agreed to abide by their demands.

Fred's first job out of college brought him to a new community where he knew no one. It was a thousand miles away from his home and from the college he had gone to. Though he did well on his job, he was alone and unhappy. He established relationships with women, but before long he discovered that these women were manipulative and extremely demanding. They insisted he do things the way they wanted them done. Fred was vulnerable and needy for relationships and he could not break them off easily. He knew this was not really what he wanted and yet, he felt that in their way, these women were providing companionship and they seemed taken with him. He chose women who were vulnerable and very needy and he was attracted to them out of a desire to rescue them—all of this to assuage his own guilt, to convince himself that he was a good guy. He also chose women, who, like his parents were demanding and manipulative. It was tempting for Fred to continue to be involved with these women and possibly to marry them, but he sensed that something was not right. And so he came for therapy.

As he began to explore his feelings, it became clear that all the women he chose were replicas of his parents. They were rigid. They had fixed ideas. Fred's feelings? Who cared? *His* feelings and thoughts were dismissed. Fred was alone and felt he was a failure. Fred was able to extricate himself from these repetitive and neurotic relationships with women once he realized his compulsion to save them. He became aware of his underlying attraction to what was familiar, though toxic, to him. He was not happy being without female companionship, but he was able to feel the pain he sustained at the hands of his parents and he was thankful that he sensed that something was wrong in his relationship with these women before he got more involved with them.

Both Valerie and Fred were able to avoid sabotaging their futures. But there was a different situation with Beatrice. Beatrice was in her thirties, living at home with her parents, holding a clerical job when she first came to me. She was an intelligent woman who had attended some courses at a local community college and done well. But she took these courses in a haphazard and sporadic manner and almost always missed deadlines for turning papers in. She was always seeking extensions and permission to take makeup examinations. She had no plans to finish college or to get a degree. As far back as elementary school, she remembered saying, "I could have done better but I'm a procrastinator. I do things in my own way and in my own time."

But she also believed that everything came harder to her and easier for others. She did not make any connection between her procrastination and vacillation and her belief that things were hard for her.

But neither was she able to see that she was caught up in a process of paralytic perfectionism. Things were harder for her because nothing she did was ever good enough. She could never allow herself to feel that something she did was finished because it could always be better. The result was that nothing got finished. She had to be above criticism, and she had to be perfect. She had few friends and her life revolved around her job and her large extended family of grandparents, parents and siblings, and nieces and nephews. And here she was, the youngest child and the only one who was not married. She was depressed and lonely and she felt she was in a rut, but saw no way out. She would begin projects only to drop them. When ideas for improving her position were suggested, she did nothing to implement them. Her parents expressed disappointment that she did not socialize more, go out with men, or show more initiative. But, they also constantly had things for her to do for them and for the rest of the family. She ran errands, did the marketing, cleaned the house, and baby-sat for the family. It was as if this was her lot in life and she passively accepted it. There was no open coercion, but there were unspoken expectations. "My mother compared me with others who were more successful. If I ever succeeded at anything, my father would disapprove and my mother would get into fights with him. Nothing I can do will please my parents, so why should I bother?"

There was another grim task creeping in from the future, and Beatrice, though she wasn't yet able to admit it, could not but help but be aware of its coming: As the youngest in this large family with her parents getting older, there was an unexpressed understanding that Beatrice would be the surrogate parent and caretaker. Instead of feeling that she was important to her family, she felt burdened with obligations that were not appreciated. Beatrice reported a dream early in therapy: "I asked my friend to sing a song. He did it. He sang three songs. I was surprised that he could sing on command." Her associations led to her feeling that she had to perform at home on command and that if she succeeded in performing on command, that others were surprised. The belief was that she could not succeed largely because she viewed the expectations of others as commands. This would arouse her passive-aggressive defenses and she wouldn't try. Another dream is instructive. "Something is stuck in my throat.

I'm coughing. Someone slapped me on the back. Overnight, I died. I had been bleeding a long time." Beatrice was choking to death. She was suppressing her feelings for a long time and a slap on the back would not relieve her feelings of strangulation. No one seemed to appreciate how deeply troubled she was and chose to dismiss her complaints as petty.

In line with "something is stuck in my throat," Beatrice commented that she was a pack rat and could not part with anything. She accumulated everything, her room was a mess, and she could not discard anything, even things for which she had absolutely no use. In addition, she reported being on a constant diet, gaining and losing weight. At times, she would eat everything in sight and once she gained weight, she would go on a rigid diet until she lost the weight. *She stuffed her feelings until she was ready to explode—and then did it all over again.* Her passive-aggressive defenses were manifested in therapy. Her aim was to parallel her frustration by creating frustration in me. She wanted to progress. But it was more important for her to go nowhere. And herein lay the dilemma—the battle between adhering to the demands of the parental status quo or acquiescing to change, that is, holding onto the strangulating and paralyzing approval of the parents or being able to transfer and identify with forces of change. Beatrice was identified with her father, a man who spent his life working long hours in a losing venture. He doggedly, stubbornly tried to prove that he could make a go of a failing business, and as he held on to it, he dragged the family down with him. Beatrice followed suit. She would take two steps forward and two steps backward going nowhere, but feeling unable to try, in a concerted way, anything new or different. Her father's defeat was her defeat and the defeat of therapy and the therapist. When she made two steps forward, her father would negate it. At the same time, he would criticize her for continuing in her path to nowhere, which placed her in the same position he was in.

Beatrice made progress, but such slow and painful progress it was hard to watch and hard to participate in. Several steps forward, many steps back. And so it is with so many who are caught up in this type of archaic repetition. The fear of offending parents, the guilt of breaking away and asserting themselves cannot be overcome easily. And for many, this expression of autonomy, which ideally occurs gradually in the course of growth, does not come at all. For others, it comes at the cost of alienation and loneliness. In families in which parents are overbearing, rigid, and strict, children grow up with fear and anxiety. The threat of guilt, punishment, the withdrawal of love and approval, and, in some cases, abandonment, force children to suppress their own needs to try things out and to make their own mistakes. Instead, they are left with constant doubts about themselves, insecurities, and unwillingness to trust their own feelings. They feel they have no choice and as we have shown, for many, they incorporate the standards and values of their parents and become little parental copies. They follow the prescribed behavior suppressing their individuality and their own creative potentials. After all, criticism is the enemy of creativity. It is a long, hard road away from such repressive and repetitive behavior.

The problem is that many of us obtain more gains out of maintaining the status quo than out of changing. We know, we feel, we want to change. We don't like the way things are, but the prospect of upsetting the stable and the familiar is too frightening. We obtain "secondary gains" to our pain and we cannot risk giving them up. I am reminded of a conference I attended on hypnosis. An elderly couple was presented. The woman walked with a walker and her husband of many years held her arm as she walked. There was nothing physically wrong with her legs or her body to explain her inability to walk. The teacher, an experienced expert in psychiatry and hypnosis, attempted to hypnotize her. She entered a trance state and he offered his suggestions that she would be able to walk. But to no avail. When she emerged from the trance, she still could not, would not, walk. The explanation was that there were too many gains to be had by having her husband cater to her, take care of her, do her bidding. Many people use infirmities to perpetuate relationships even at the expense of freedom and autonomy. Satisfactions are derived by being limited and crippled physically or psychologically. This is often one of the greatest deterrents to progress in psychotherapy. It is unconscious, but more gratification is derived by perpetuating this state of affairs than by giving them up. Beatrice, for all of her unhappiness, was fearful of relinquishing her place in the family. She felt needed, and she felt threatened by the thought of achieving anything that would have contributed to a greater sense of independence and self. The risks were too great, the loss of the known and familiar was too frightening.

Residing in all of us is a child who wants to experiment with the new and the different, a child who has a healthy curiosity about the world around him, who wants to learn and to create. In all of us are needs for security, certainty, and stability. Ideally, there develops a balance between the two types of needs. The base of security is present and serves as a foundation which allows the exploration of new ideas and new learning and experimenting. But all too often, the security and dependency needs outweigh the freedom to explore and we stifle, even snuff out, the creative urges, the fantasy, the child in us. We seek the sources that fill our dependency and security needs at the expense of the curious, imaginative child.

There are those who take too many risks, who take too many chances and lose, to the detriment of all concerned. But there are others who are risk-averse and do little with their talents and abilities for fear of having to change their view of themselves as being the child, the dependent one, the protected one. Autonomy, independence, success are scary because they mean we can no longer justify our needs to be protected. Success to these people does not breed success. Success breeds more work, more dependence, more reason to give up the rationales for moving on, away from, and exploring the new and the different.

Chapter 2

Repetitions in Marriage: Unwritten Contracts and Complementary Repetitions

Love. Everyone wants it. Everyone needs it. Epic poems have been written about it. Soaring operas and simple melodies have been sung to it. Individuals have been known to kill for it. It is the one thing that no one can live without.

But what exactly is this thing called love? Who can really define it? Is it an emotion, a pure feeling of selflessness and commitment to the well-being of another, akin to a religious experience? Or is it a kind of madness? There is, I think, some truth to be gleaned from phrases commonly used to describe this thing called love: "*Madly* in love, *crazy* about her, *insanely* jealous." Perhaps those phrases indicate an unconscious recognition that love is a kind of madness, a state of mind out of the ordinary, a lapse in judgment or common sense. Certainly, no one who "falls in love" stands back, at least for a time, to examine it, to ask what it is. One knows absolutely and for certain when one has fallen in love.

However, what we call love is sometimes not love at all. Rather, love—and consequently marriages—is almost always made with an unconscious expectation that one partner will fill the other partner's unmet needs and even provide a sense of wholeness. It is what I call the unwritten contract, present in almost all marriages. This perception or motive is rarely made explicit, because the individual is rarely aware of it. Instead, he or she is aware only of loving this other person.

Is this a bad thing, this wish to have one's needs met? Of course not. In any marriage or partnership, we seek to have our needs fulfilled and to fill, where possible, the needs of our partners. If the perceptions and expectations are realistic, the marriage can develop and thrive, because we are clear in what we want and how we hope to get it.

But those are not the marriages of which I speak here. The failure in many marriages, shown by the appalling divorce rate, is not that conscious, wholesome need or desire. Rather the problem is the *unconscious* expectations of one or both partners, expectations that are unrealistic and distorted. It is these couples who are doomed to become yet another divorce statistic.

Is it really possible that one can be so unaware of one's needs, so much so that a spouse is turned into nothing more than a hope for the impossible? Is it possible that there are individuals who are so deprived and unwelcome in their birth families that they spend their growing years looking for unconditional parental love—and expect to get it from a spouse?

Unfortunately, sadly, it is not only possible, but it happens all too often. That wish and many others are played out in the cycle of repeat marriages. There are those who grew up in fractured homes who look for a partner who will provide them with the sense of stability that they never knew in their growing-up families—only to be disappointed when the spouse in unable to provide that for which they long. One seeks repeatedly what one did not have. Why then does it all seem to go wrong? It goes wrong when the individual simply perpetuates those early losses, repeating the tragedy of the past. And here is the scary part—scary and true: Though almost never apparent at first glance, the repetition comes in the form of *marrying* the harsh and demanding or cold and unresponsive mother or father. Sometimes, over and over again. Why would anyone do that?

When I meet with a couple for marital therapy, my practice at the first or second session is to ask them to describe their mothers and fathers. Often, in fact almost always, in the course of therapy that follows, I begin to see a clear fit between the spouse and one or the other of the parents. What's even more tragic is that the parent who is most similar to the spouse is also the parent with whom the patient had the most difficulty. The harsh and cold father is repeated in the harsh husband or wife. The strict and domineering and unforgiving mother is repeated in the strict and domineering spouse. This represents the acting out of unresolved relationships with the parent who was perceived as the aggressor, the parent the patient could not get to fulfill his or her needs. The unconscious choice of the mate represents an attempt to *change this parent*, to get the love and caring that was missing. The spouse in turn, fills the role of the one who frustrates. The result is complaints such as "He doesn't hear me; that's not what I said; that's not what I meant." This in turn leads to power struggles, battles of wills, fights about who's right and who's wrong. What follows sometimes is that quiet, but intensely unpeaceful feeling of walking on egg shells in order not to upset the balance. The couple is playing a duet, claiming to want harmony, but instead, playing dissonances.

Sometimes, there is a dim awareness of what is taking place, fleeting thoughts that the spouse is behaving in ways reminiscent of the frustrating parent, but those thoughts are frequently brushed aside. Because we fail to recognize the dynamics of the interaction with the spouse, and because we don't fully remember the harmful impact the parent had on us, we tend to repeat the relationship again and again. We expect, we hope, that this time we will succeed in getting what we want. We live with the hope and expectation that we will find the fulfillment in marriage that we have not found until now. If we sense that the potential or the actual spouse cannot meet out expectations, we live with the fiction that we will get them to be more responsive, more giving, stronger, kinder, less harsh. Why? Because we continue to be caught up in the childhood fantasy that we will be able to please and change the parent, that we will be able to get the parents to love us as we need to be loved. In many instances, this kind of thinking and wishing did not work with our parents. And almost certainly, it will not work in marriage.

Marriages are made in the unconscious, and never was this more apparent to me than when I consulted with Jillian and Michael.

When Jillian arrived alone one spring afternoon, she put out a well-manicured hand to greet me and sat in the chair across from me, bright looking, tastefully dressed, and exceedingly attractive. Her voice was well modulated, and she had no trouble expressing her concerns, the concern that had brought her to me—her twelve-year-old son who was having difficulties in school. Testing had revealed that he had a high IQ, but he was not performing well. Jillian was self-aware enough to wonder if tensions in her marriage did not have something to do with his school behavior. It took only one session for Jillian to move away from the issue of her son (which essentially turned out to be a nonissue) and to begin discussing her marital difficulties. She had been married to her husband, Michael, for sixteen years and she was fed up with the relationship. "He's such a great guy, bright and honest and good looking," she told me, when she first spoke of him. "But he's plodding, slow. I want to light a fire under him to get him to move on with his life. He's had this job for years. It pays barely enough to make ends meet and there's no future there for him. He knows it, too. But does it bother him? No!"

"But it bothers you," I suggested.

"You can believe it does. I'm an office manager, but I'm constantly on the lookout for a better job, always networking. I want to make more of my life, I want to earn more money and have a more responsible job that's valued. I want to effect changes. Michael is ethical and honest. He's capable, very capable. But he has no drive at all. At all! Even my getting upset doesn't seem to bother him. He says it's all right, it's going to be all right. Well, how can he just say that when things aren't good?"

"Does he get angry when you bug him about it?"

"Angry? Him? He can't even get angry. I would admire him more if he did. And he's a smart guy, too, very well read. And this is weird—he has a lot of friends. People like him. But he's driving me crazy. He procrastinates. Over everything. He can't even get up and change a light bulb the day I ask him to. It can take him a month to do such a trivial thing."

"And how does he feel about your son and his grades in school?"

She made a face and shrugged. "It's fine with him. He has no strong feelings about anything!"

I thought this might be a good time to ask about their sexual relationship. In many marriages, the sexual life is a good barometer of the rest of the relationship and often indicates what is going on between the partners.

"Sex?" she replied. "He rarely approaches me for sex. When we try, he loses his erection. I've urged him to see a doctor about this, and like everything else, he agrees. But does he do anything about it? No. It's as if he doesn't care even about this. What kind of a man is that? And if I initiate sex, it's even worse. Then he can't function at all."

"It's always been this way?" I asked.

"No." She became thoughtful then. "No. It's gotten worse. He's so passive about everything. Honestly, sometimes I think I married my mother."

This was the opening for which I had been waiting, the opportunity to explore the dynamics of her birth family and how it was acted out in this, her marriage. It was interesting to see the parallels and, also, to see how the dynamics were acted out in therapy with me.

We began by working together, just Jillian and me. During the course of individual therapy, some interesting parallels emerged. Jillian's mother was an opinionated woman who was critical of her daughter while clearly favoring her son, Jillian's brother and only sibling. Mother found fault with almost everything her daughter did. She demeaned her place in the family, a view that Jillian attributed, correctly, to her mother favoring the male child.

"She always told me how disorganized I was and that it was time I got my act together," Jillian told me. "She was active in the family and in the community and she seemed to care about us—but she only cared if she could run everything, including my life. She wanted to know everything I thought and felt. So then, I'd confide in her, and next thing I knew, she'd broadcast everything I told her to the whole world. I always felt betrayed. But then, stupid me, a week later, I would go back and confide again. She was so controlling! Yet, and this is the odd thing, she was so submissive to these irrational demands my father would make of her."

"Irrational?" I asked.

"You better believe it. He had an explosive temper, and if he came home in a bad mood, watch out! He tore into my mother and my brother. He was never mean to me, but I was afraid that I'd be the next one for him to scream at."

I found that an interesting observation, and urged Jillian to pursue that line of thought. It came out, in small and big ways, that Jillian thought little of herself as a person. She did not think she was bright or capable, but she knew she was pretty and she thought this was her only attribute. She was coquettish, attracting men, but not letting them get close to her. She was afraid of men, and it seemed, she had good reason to be. She was terrified of her father's violent temper and lived in fear that some day he would turn his rage toward her. There were sexual overtones to his relationship with Jillian, who had to stave this off by being Daddy's pretty and cute little girl.

This family constellation was reenacted in her relationship with me. Jillian managed to discover a good deal about my home life and clearly wanted to get closer to me personally. She was quite inventive and persistent in confronting me about events and the people in my private life. While she knew it was inappropriate, she seemed unable to stop what she was doing. This grew out of some of the same issues that were operating in the marriage and represented a repetition of her earlier life. She was in awe of me and what I knew about her. She feared that I, like her mother, would criticize her and use what I knew about her to hurt her. She feared my getting angry with her, and she had to aggrandize herself in my eyes. By investigating my personal life, she felt she had some power over me to even the playing field. While not openly competitive, she had to feel that she had some control over the situation. And she had to show me how wonderful she was, in spite of her feelings of inferiority.

"A young good-looking guy came into the office yesterday and told me that I was beautiful and I should have been a model and he admired the clothes I wore."

When I did not respond to such statements, she became silent and withdrawn, brooding. As the therapy moved along, she began to have repeated concerns about her vision. She maintained she could not see well, and she feared losing her vision. Several visits to a variety of ophthalmologists revealed that her vision was unimpaired. Yet she continued to fear.

Would it be too much to say that there were issues emerging that she did not want to see or become aware of? Interesting, because as our work progressed, her fears of visual loss disappeared. However, something new began to happen: She became angry, furious at me because her eyes were being opened and she did not want that. She did not want to see her role in perpetuating the problems with Michael that she complained about. She did not want to see that she was compelled to be the one in command, the top dog, just as her mother had tried to be in command. By being in command, by demanding that Michael "get a move on and do something with his life," she was ignoring her own underlying feelings of neediness and vulnerability. She was fearful of owning up to her needs for closeness and intimacy and repressed such feelings in order to convince herself that she was in control—yet at other times, she seemed to want me to take care of her and solve her problems. In the next session, she often acted as though she needed me not at all. As a child, she had not made the gradual transition that most children make, from the needy little person who craves and truly needs and deserves support, to the independent, assertive adult. In therapy, all those contradictions were acted out. I was a pain because I was the parent to the confused child in her. Or, alternately, I represented the needy child and she had to show me that she truly did not need me. Or anyone.

There was no in-between in her inner life, or in her outer life. And I was the one who brought this conflict into sharp relief.

This same conflict was constantly acted out in the marriage. She would complain that Michael did not do enough to take care of her, while at other times she would not accept any of his efforts to do for her.

This conflict, over-dependence and independence, was acted out in the sexual area. She could be seductive when she chose and she could decide how far things should go. She would allow intimacy only to the point that Michael began to feel that he was functioning sexually and then she would undermine him. (She was in control.) She could demean Michael for his lack of initiative and his failure to function sexually. (She was in control.) As in everything else, when Michael showed initiative, his efforts were undermined and he gave up. However, she had sexual fantasies in which she was the masochistic object of the sadistic and overpowering male. Thus, she repressed her submissive and passive-dependent fantasies and acted out her more aggressive, controlling, and sadistic-seductive impulses.

Essentially, the unwritten contract here was one in which Jillian could love a man who gave her the outward appearance of success, of being an upstanding person in the community, a person who would not be criticized or found lacking. At the same time, she needed to defend herself in her personal life by being in control, by not showing vulnerabilities, by avoiding intimacies that might expose her submissive urges. She sabotaged the very conditions that she yearned for consciously, a partner who was successful, self-confident, and active. But this would have violated Jillian's part of the contract. She needed to stave off the critical opinionated mother who submitted to the father. She had to stave off the harsh, angry, and gruff father. The repetition here was in the form of assuring herself that she would *not* be in the position she was in her primary family, by doing the opposite. She had to be beyond criticism, the one who was in charge. Vulnerability and neediness had to be avoided at all costs.

Again, this was all acted out in the therapeutic relationship. She sought my approval by demonstrating how busy she was, what wonderful things she did in the office, what initiatives she took, and by bolstering herself at the expense of others, especially her husband.

Eventually, due to Jillian's hard work and the success of the sometimes difficult therapeutic relationship, there came the time when Jillian's eyes were open, and she was not only able to see what was happening, but able to make some decisions. She realized that she was sabotaging opportunities for a more fulfilling life and she finally came to the point of accepting this consciously. It was now a matter of choice to stay with Michael, not necessity. She had alternatives.

Meanwhile, what was Michael's part in this process? At my urging, as well as Jillian's urging, Michael entered therapy with a very good therapist whom I had recommended. Michael kept to his scheduled appointments, but it seemed after several months, both to Michael and to his therapist, that not much progress was being made. At the time, I had a good therapy group in progress and suggested that perhaps this would be an appropriate place for Michael to work out some of his problems. At the very least, it would be a place for him to learn, in a structured, safe environment, how he was viewed by others, not just by Jillian.

And so, for a time, Michael worked with both the group and with me individually. It was here that Michael's background came into full view, his history and his view of himself. Perhaps nothing contributes more to a man's view of himself than his father's view of him, extending back to earliest childhood. It quickly became obvious, that while Jillian married a man who was not like her father, who was, in fact, the antithesis of her father, Michael married *his* father in Jillian. Michael's father was an immature, self-obsessed, and insecure man, concerned with himself and his business, constantly aggrandizing himself. He made sure that Michael knew he could never live up to his father's expectations and could never be as successful as he was. Michael was set up to be a disappointment to his father, and his father took every opportunity to make sure that happened.

Some men and boys would react aggressively to such treatment. Michael, however, never fought back and it became clear almost from our very first meeting. The only expression of resentment came out in words to me such as, "I never want to be like my father. I don't want to look like him. I don't want to act like him. Nothing!" As his father took no pride in Michael, Michael took no pride in his father.

"My father told me from the time I was a kid that I'd never make much of my life, that I couldn't do anything right," Michael said at one of our first meetings. "I never got any support or affirmation from him. It was as if no matter what I did, it wasn't good enough. Not only that, he *expected* me to fail, before I even tried anything."

"Even as a little kid?" I asked.

Michael nodded. "Even as a little kid," he said. "I was so intimidated by him. He was always telling me how useless and stupid I was. It got so that I'd do anything to avoid being told that. I remember one time, I was just little, six, I think, and I fell out of a tree and broke my leg. It was agonizing. But I didn't tell my dad, or my mom, either. I knew my father especially would tell me how stupid I was. Finally, about two days later, when I couldn't stand the pain anymore, could hardly even walk, they realized something was wrong and took me to a doctor. I had a broken leg."

"And what happened then?" I asked.

He shrugged. "My dad said I was stupid and clumsy. And on top of that, he was mad at me for not telling him for two days."

Yes, I could see how that would have happened. His father had no clue that he had set the stage for his son to be so fearful that he couldn't even confide his pain to him.

"So you gave up? Didn't even try?" I suggested.

"Well, no, I did try. For a while. I tried so much to gain his approval. I remember one time, I was in highschool then, I worked really, really hard to get into a good school. An Ivy League one. And I did!"

"And?"

"And he said we couldn't afford it. So I went to a state school instead."

"*Could* he have afforded it?" I asked.

Michael shrugged, then nodded. "Maybe. I mean, we could. It might have been hard. But I was willing to work hard and help out. I was always willing to work hard."

"Why do you think your father did that to you?" I asked.

Michael shrugged. He smiled. For a long time, he said nothing. I let the silence go on, hoping that in the quiet, Michael might experience, and uncover, even a hint of what was going on under the surface. Instead, the silence just stretched on and on.

Silence, as has been noted, can be an important tool in the psychotherapeutic process. In the quiet, the individual often remembers events, and, even more, feels the emotions that attach to those events. If a therapist is tuned in, is understanding and willing to let that silence go on, many things can be learned. The therapist might see tears forming, might get a glimpse of something so subtle as a headshake. And a simple question or statement can bring release and relief to the open. "You seem afraid," or even "What are you thinking?" can be an opening, and the individual can often experience and release those deeply painful, unconscious memories.

This did not happen with Michael. He seemed quite content with the silence. What's more, I could see that there was nothing bubbling away beneath the surface; no anger, no tears, not even much hostility. There was just a pathetic kind of waiting, a sense that nothing mattered much. I realized then that this therapeutic relationship had quickly become a repetition of what had gone on with his father in his early life. Michael responded to any challenge or question that might bring insight with a shrug, with silence. He felt that it was inevitable that whatever he tried, whatever he did, he would fail. So why try? Why bother? His solution to the dilemma was to emotionally detach, to have no inkling about his true feelings.

I learned then that Michael had entered therapy once before at Jillian's behest and it had failed. It seemed that this time, with me, he was also determined to fail, to undermine any progress or any insights. He was pleasant. But he wasn't going to try. It was clear to me that Michael was depressed despite his outward show of conviviality. And the reason he was depressed was that he was furious. His anger was turned inward. He could not allow himself to express or even to experience his anger. So he took his anger out on himself. He withdrew from situations that made him angry by developing passive-aggressive defenses. When he was asked to look at himself in therapy, he withdrew. And so it went on. I thought—hoped—it would change. I used every therapeutic device I knew. But things in therapy only became worse. Michael no longer retreated into silence. Instead, he did something worse: he began to agree. *Yes, he could see that. Yes, that was true. Yes, I see what you mean. I can see how that might be.* But they were words only. If they were indeed insights, they were insights that he would do nothing about.

Outside the consulting room, I discovered that he had other ways of negotiating his way through life. He would help and cooperate with others, especially if he were given menial or technical tasks, more as a way of getting others off his back than out of any desire to win approval or to seek praise. He would never say no, stoically and reluctantly going along with demands made of him. Often, however, his agreement meant nothing. He would procrastinate, get caught up in perfectionism that was paralyzing. Very little got accomplished. (Remember, he couldn't even change a light bulb.)

But conversely, he'd become very involved in tasks that he was good at and that he enjoyed. This was acted out in his relationship to Jillian where he became a general handyman. This contributed to Jillian's admiration for him, but the admiration was based upon his being a good handyman or "techy."

"Jillian had trouble with the computer in the office and called me. I went over there and in no time, I got it up and running. She was so happy and so was her boss. It made me feel good."

So there, he could succeed in tiny ways, insignificant ways. But in major areas of his life, he could not stand up for himself. He could not make demands for himself or seek rewards for himself and his efforts. He felt he was damaged, impotent, and inadequate and that whatever he did, it would never be good enough.

The discrepancy noted earlier between Jillian's submissive fantasies and her seductive-sadistic behavior was complemented in the situation with Michael. His sexual fantasies were replete with aggressive and sadistic themes, but he acted out the submissive, passive part in overt behavior. The fantasies represented the repressed and inhibited urges that could not be expressed overtly. If Michael could have accessed, experienced, and expressed his anger, he might have been able to resolve his dilemma. His anger could have been harnessed and used productively to his advantage, and he could have been very successful.

I commented to Michael on several occasions, "It sounds as if you're really angry, but it seems hard for you to be able to face these feelings. You're taking your anger out on yourself by repeatedly feeling as if you're going to be defeated regardless of what you say or do."

Michael nodded. "Right. Right." He agreed. He did nothing about it. It was too dangerous and risky for him to do so.

Michael's paralysis and his frustration were paralleled in the paralysis and frustration of myself as his therapist, not only in the individual sessions, but also later in group therapy. I believed that in a group, Michael could get a clearer idea of how he was viewed, not just by me or by Jillian, but by a group of sensitive individuals who were willing to help and to be helped. But there too, Michael frustrated every effort. He dragged his feet, got caught up in details, and derailed efforts to move him off the position he was in. He dealt with issues by going around in circles, undermining efforts by me and by the group to get to central issues. Group members pointed out to him what he was doing and expressed their frustration at his not doing things to help himself. Did this help? No. On the contrary, to Michael this was but one more indication that he was a failure. This too was interpreted to him, but to no avail.

It was painful to see this happening, painful to see Michael, with all of his unrealized potential, placing himself in situations that perpetuated his problems, undermining efforts to bring about change. It was painful to see him continually acting *in response to his father*, sabotaging his treatment as he sabotaged other aspects of his life. For most men, the time comes to symbolically bury the father, mourn his passing, and then move on. Michael could not do this. He kept his father alive through his own self-sabotaging behavior.

Just as Jillian chose to marry Michael because he did not threaten her with his anger, assuring her that she would not be criticized and demeaned, so Michael chose to marry Jillian. She would keep him in a state of impotence and protect him from venting his rage. Michael knew what he was dealing with in his relationship with Jillian, just as he was familiar with the relationship he had with his father. As painful as it was, at least it was familiar, a known quantity and he could not wish for much more. Much of Michael's life was devoted to avoiding and evading confrontations that might trigger expressions of his anger because he was so fearful of the emergence of this anger. Jillian unconsciously imposed limits on his experiencing a sense of strength and confidence. She knocked him down as soon as he started to get up, so to speak. Michael proved to himself in this relationship that his father was right, that he really was a failure, disappointing and inept.

Further, by repeating his traumatic relationship with his father through Jillian, he attempted to tame the beast. He would try to win approval, always knowing that his efforts would be in vain. Unconsciously, he was attempting to gain control over the rejection, but repeatedly proving to himself that this would never happen. Michael was caught up in a self-sabotaging repetition. His admiration for Jillian and her accomplishments represented his vicarious identification with the aggressor without placing himself at risk.

However, and this became more obvious the longer I worked with Michael, by his behavior, he was also proving something else. He was withholding success from his father and from Jillian, so that they would get no pride from being related to him. In his own way, he communicated that he was basically a capable person who could do more than he did, but even at his own expense, he would give them no satisfaction by doing so. Rejection was what he knew and was familiar with.

And so, in the end, Michael preferred living with that, rather than taking the chance of doing more himself only to fail. In spite of all of our efforts, his included, Michael would not, maybe *could* not, budge from the place where he had been put by his father, and the place he had ultimately chosen for himself.

And so, what became of that marriage? Was it a happily-ever-after story?

Yes.

And no.

There are times when basic conflicts and traumas that occur early in life are so severe that they cannot be undone. The result is that some individuals, Michael, Jillian, for example, make compromises that limit their potentials, but that they are willing to accept. They choose to compromise rather than fight an uphill battle. There is sometimes an awareness that the gains from maintaining the status quo are greater than the price that would be paid for change—because change would also mean upheaval. But this is the important point: *There is a major difference between being in difficult situations that recur without one having any awareness of what is happening and the recognition that one has alternatives and could effect changes in such self-sabotaging behavior.* The difference, the vital difference, is in the recognition. Freud has written, "As a matter of fact I've always known it; only I've never thought of it."[1] It is but another way of commenting on all of these unwritten, unconscious contracts.

Jillian could have changed her situation if she were willing to accept the consequences. She chose not to disrupt her marriage and family life despite the fact that limitations were placed upon what she could expect. She had a choice of freeing herself from a marriage to an attractive, honest, caring—although passive—husband and finding a more assertive, aggressive man. She chose the first. She accepted Michael as he was and stopped provoking him and demeaning him.

At one of our last sessions, she said, "Things with Michael are not going to change. I've tried and tried and maybe I've made things worse by pestering him to do more and be more and by pushing him away when he tries to get close. But now I know he's not going to change. But I don't want to leave him. I guess I need him this way. I do love him and he's good to me. It would be too much of an upheaval to throw this marriage into turmoil after all these years. So this is the way things will be and that will be all right with me."

By that time, we had spent many hours together on this journey and there had been much growth. I felt comfortable commenting to her, "You seem to need the relationship with Michael the way it is. You have changed. He has tried to change. But overall, he has been there for you. Perhaps you can live with that now, knowing what you know."

She agreed. And so the marriage survived because Jillian came to the recognition that changing the conditions of the unwritten contract would have come at too high a cost. It would have threatened the very foundations of the marriage. She chose not to do it, and she was willing to pay the price. It was a clear, conscious decision based upon years of hard work in psychotherapy. The result was that Jillian did not act out of unknown motives. She had the freedom to choose based upon her understanding of herself and her situation.

I make it clear to couples when they first come to me because of marital difficulties that the goal of therapy is not to save or to destroy their marriage. Rather, the goal is to enable the individuals to become aware of what caused the present difficulties in the first place and to enhance their understanding of themselves.

"If, by knowing yourself better and appreciating your role in the difficulty, this improves the marriage, that's fine," I tell them. "But divorce is a calculated risk when entering marital therapy." And I follow that caution by reminding them that there is nothing to be gained by leaving one marriage only to remarry someone with whom the same pattern will be repeated. It happens all too often.

How many times have we had a friend or acquaintance introduce us to a new second or third spouse only to find startling similarities in personality between the new "love" and the old one?

Which brings me to Joel.

Joel married five times and divorced four times. He married, divorced, and then remarried the *same* woman twice. If it weren't so sad, one could laugh and say that he seemed to be a glutton for punishment.

"I'm looking for a woman who is warm and caring and I always seem to end up with cold, distant, domineering, and rejecting women," he told me, the first time we met. "They seem great when I date and court them, but once into the marriage, they change. They're not the person I went out with."

I learned that Joel showered these women with expensive gifts, trips, and homes. He was the sugar daddy. After a while though, he would begin to feel that he was being used, taken for what he could give and getting little in return. "I'm only good for paying the bills, but I get no appreciation or affection. It's not like it was at the beginning of the relationship. This happens with all of them," he said.

"And what does your wife say about that?" I asked, though I was tempted to ask, "What have *all* of your wives said about that?" Because it was already clear to me that Joel too was in a major repetitive cycle.

"Oh, just that it's all that I give. She says I only want to dominate, to be the big shot. She says I'm not interested in her as a person."

At our second session, I asked if Joel would bring his wife to a session. I did not intend for this to be marital therapy—Joel had made it clear that he did not want that—but I did want to get a sense for what this fifth wife was seeing.

"Socially, he's so personable and everyone likes him," she said, with some despair. "But he doesn't give of himself. Everything is superficial, everything is an exchange. He doesn't say it openly, but it's clear that since he has the money and gives material things, he expects that he should dictate everything else. I feel I have no input, that I'm not taken seriously. All of my concerns are dismissed."

"Not all of them," Joel said, grinning.

She just glared at him, but soon broke into a smile.

I could see why. Joel was charming. He was personable. He had a good sense of humor. He once wore to a session a T-shirt that read, "My wife says I don't listen. At least I think that's what she said." But the sad truth was that he didn't listen. He didn't give love. Because somewhere in his privileged background, he had been taught not to.

As it was revealed later in our work together, as a child, Joel's sense of self-worth came strictly from his accomplishments.

He was very intelligent and got high marks in school. He was praised.

In high school, he was an outstanding debater. He was praised.

He went on to a top law school where he used that talent. He was praised.

He was also multitalented and a very good musician. There, too, he was praised.

However, he was never asked by his parents how he felt. He was never asked how he was getting along with friends or teachers. He was never—never once, he told me—told that he was loved. He was praised for his accomplishments. What did love have to do with it?

Nothing. And so Joel repeated this in his marriages. His entire adult life was spent in a desperate search for someone who cared for and loved him for himself. He longed for that. He longed deeply for it. But he didn't know how to get it. Instead, he acted on the belief that he could only win love by demonstrating the things he could *do*, the material things he could *give*. He yearned for someone to love him for himself, but he didn't know how to give of himself. So he kept making the same mistakes again and again, seeking love by winning, succeeding, being outstanding; seeking love by buying it in one way or the other. The result was that his wives felt that all they could get from him was "things," so they took them and wanted more and more to replace what was lacking in terms of relatedness. Joel, in turn, felt he was being taken advantage of. This only convinced him of what he already believed—that the only thing he had to offer was "things" and no woman could really love him for himself.

The problems that Joel had are good examples of his unconsciously relating to others as his parents related to him. He identified with his parents and treated others as he was treated. He was so used to this that he took for granted that everyone interacted on the basis of accomplishments and material things. But Joel was smart. He knew something was wrong and his track record with women proved it. And so he came to me.

Change in psychotherapy is based largely on having a concerned, caring, and consistent relationship with the therapist. It means taking the therapeutic process seriously, sticking with it, allowing the therapist to become part of one's life, and incorporating changes through internalizing the process. Psychotherapy provides an opportunity to relate to someone who cares, who tries to understand, who tries to facilitate changes in the way in which one sees oneself and one's place in the world. At first, Joel tried to dismiss repeated lateness to sessions because of his busy schedule. He claimed that his repeated business trips, which interrupted the therapeutic process, were far more important than our work together. He had no qualms about this and dismissed my concerns.

"I'll pay you for the time. So why should it be an issue?" he asked.

I'll pay you for your time.

Hadn't I picked up on this formulation before, in relation to his wives—all five of them? And because therapists are human, I also found myself responding inside to the same cry that his wife had expressed earlier to me: he doesn't give of himself. *"Everything is superficial,"* she had said. *"Everything is an exchange. He doesn't say it openly, but it's clear that since he has the money and gives material things, he should dictate everything else. I have no input, I'm not taken seriously. All of my concerns are dismissed."*

And so, I fed back to him the feelings that he touched off in me.

"You make me feel," I said, "as if I can be bought and sold. You make me feel as if I am a commodity and that this relationship is totally dispensable. Yes, this is a fee-based relationship, but the money is not the issue. The issue is that you're throwing roadblocks in the path of what you say you want and need. By dismissing this on the basis that you'll pay for the time shows that relationships can be bought and sold. It shows that relationships mean nothing to you. And perhaps this is the problem in your relationships with women."

Joel was incredulous. I had used the feelings that he touched off in me as a barometer of what he triggered in women and reflected this back to him.

With good results. Perhaps because he was willing to change, perhaps because he was also very bright, he began to see what he hadn't been able to see for his entire life. He saw, and it became an epiphany of the way in which he handled relationships in his life. It showed that someone was attuned to him and felt for him. Gradually,

Joel changed. He became more giving and more responsive. There was more give and take, more reciprocity in therapy and outside. Marriage number five has—so far—been successful.

The need to protect and defend against hurt, especially following repeated hurts and rejections, can sabotage the very things we want. Jay had been living with Martha for years. They both had been recoiling from failed marriages. Jay believed that he finally had found in Martha someone who could be warm and responsive to him. Instead, due to events with the children of her first marriage, she became cold and distant and angry. She virtually shut off communication with Jay. He reached a point of suffering so much hurt that he could not go on, and he came to consult with me.

When Martha discovered that Jay was seeing a therapist, she became extremely threatened. She insisted that they had to work out their difficulties between the two of them. Jay, however, recognized that this could not happen when Martha refused to discuss anything with him. After Jay had had several sessions with me, Martha grudgingly agreed to come with him to a session. During that time, she did not say much, but she did ask Jay to give the relationship more time. In subsequent weeks, Jay related that she had begun to talk more and to be more responsive to him.

However, after just a few weeks of this, Jay came to a session saying that he wanted to leave her. After months of begging her to be more open and giving to him, she was giving the very thing he wanted—yet he was ready to leave.

"I don't see a future for the two of us," he said.

I asked Jay why, asked him to think about what he was saying.

He thought for a time, and then responded, "When something starts to go right, I don't want to get hurt again. I was hurt so many times and for so long, I'm afraid to take a chance." And this despite the fact that Martha was making it clear that she wanted this relationship to work, that she was beginning to let down her defensive barriers.

Martha was closed off through silence—and Jay withdrew by creating internal scenarios when he was afraid to communicate. He wanted closeness and warmth, but he was also fearful of upsetting her and did not speak up. He would not confront her with his feelings, especially his anger at her for rejecting his efforts. Theirs was a parent-child relationship in which Jay was compelled to please mother in exchange for the hope of winning love. Martha was the cold and unresponsive parent. Jay inhibited his feelings and stewed about them while growing further and further from his wife. Finally, when Martha was ready to open up, Jay had created so much rage and defensiveness that he was going to spurn her—gain revenge—and undermine a chance to work things out.

This relationship points to another problem in the way individuals react to trauma. The breakdown in communication, so often presented as the reason for problems in relationships, is in reality part of the defensive structure in response to trauma. It is not only a breakdown in verbal communication, but in emotional communication as well. There is a numbing of feelings and responsiveness. *If you won't reach out to me, why should I reach out to you?* The result is that the relationship is one of tentativeness, one where each individual feels the need to tread lightly, to avoid anything troublesome or real. Out of fear of reprisal, out of fear of one's own anger, the tendency is to withdraw, to shut down both verbally and nonverbally.

"She gives me the silent treatment" is a commonly heard complaint. "We live like two ships passing in the night." This state of alienation is based upon fears that the partner will get angry if the other person expresses how he feels. This fear is also expressed in terms of fragility, "I can't say anything because she'll fall apart, she's so sensitive." So the distancing continues and gets worse and worse.

Not expressing one's feelings and reactions in words leads in turn to not expressing feelings in behavior and in emotional reactions. "Why should I express how I feel? He won't hear me anyway. It won't make a bit of difference." "I can't talk to her. Everything falls on deaf ears." These are the refrains of broken relationships based upon fear and withdrawal, a state of resignation based upon repeated hurts.

Can this change? Could it change with Jay and Martha? If one partner can risk his fears and can recognize that the standoff is due to avoidance of aggression and of hurt, then the barrier of silence can begin to break down.

Jay came to one session saying, "I told her that I'm not a mind reader. Unless she tells me what she's feeling or thinking, I have no way of knowing."

This is the kind of response that can lead to change. This is also the kind of reaction that is unthinkable in the midst of emotional standoffs. The realization that the fear of anger and the fear of fragility are carry-overs from earlier traumatic relationships is necessary.

She's not my mother who practically fainted if I spoke back to her.

He's not my father whose looks could kill if I expressed my feelings.

By coming to this recognition, one is able to change present relationships—unless, of course, one unconsciously married a partner who is very similar to one's parent!

The compulsion to repeat is a form of acting out a trauma through destructive behavior, though almost always the individual is completely unaware that this is what he or she is doing. Moreover, "overdetermined" is the term we use when such destructive behavior is prompted by a *multitude* of factors of which the individual is not aware. This was amply shown when Louis came to me, so clear that even Louis may have had some hint within himself of what was happening. Perhaps, though I suspect that Louis would have denied it at the time, somewhere deep inside, he was absolutely sure that something beyond his control was driving him.

When we first talked, I learned that Louis had been married for ten years and had just begun moving toward divorce. He had hired a lawyer, and was taking some steps financially to bring this marriage to an end. He did not want to discuss or examine what was driving him to this decision. He simply knew that he had to divorce, and though he came to me for counseling, he made it quite clear that he was leaving the marriage. It had become suffocating.

So if not the marriage problem, what was he here for?

Well, other things were on his mind. And as he filled in his background for me, I learned these things: Louis's father had left when Louis was small, abandoning him, his sister, and their mother. I also learned that not only had Louis's father left when Louis was young, but his father's father, his grandfather, had also left the family when *his* son was small. Now Louis was about to repeat the pattern. Was this mere coincidence? Or was something more insidious at work here? I couldn't help thinking that Louis was announcing: "My grandfather left his family; my father left his family; I must leave my family."

Was this decision based upon a sense that the marriage had to end anyway, so it might as well be gotten over with now? The marriage has to die so why wait? Now, one could rationalize that indeed this compulsion was based, not on a repetitive impulse, but on facts, for certainly there were problems within this marriage, and the biggest seemed to be his wife, Virginia, constantly checking up on him. After all, who does want to feel constrained, checked-up on, monitored every minute of every day?

But was that really what was going on? Was that the core of the problem? Although reluctant to talk about it at first, gradually Louis felt comfortable enough to explore at least some of the marriage situation. He was especially irate about his wife, Virginia, constantly keeping tabs on him, calling him frequently on the job, wanting to know where he went and what he did, demanding an accounting for every hour in the day. He felt smothered. He had no time for himself, he complained, he was under constant surveillance and he had to get out. They had a baby, and he felt overwhelmed with responsibilities. "I can't even go fishing!" he exclaimed. "When I do, Virginia complains that I'm neglecting her and the baby. And the checking up on me every moment is just getting to me."

"Why do you think she checks up on you the way she does?" I asked.

Louis shrugged. He had no idea. And yet, as he went on talking, he began to share that he wasn't always honest with her. He would not come home from his office when he said he would. There were even nights when he would not come home at all. Worse, he refused to account for those absences to Virginia. Could he really be so dim that he did not see that he was provoking her reactions?

Of course, it was natural to ask what had happened when Louis's father had left him as a child, and Louis seemed happy to talk about that, relieved, even. His mother, he said, had naturally felt abandoned.

But she also, (quite *un*naturally, I thought) made a point of impressing on Louis that he owed it to her to be the good son. She and Louis hated the father for abandoning them and they joined together in the feelings of rejection. It was then that Louis felt he had to take over for his father, providing his mother with solace and rescue. He did what she wanted, and, all too often, had to forego having the fun and freedom that his friends had. If he wanted to go to a football game, his mother would become suddenly ill, and need him at home. If he had a sleepover at a friend's house, she needed him to run errands for her that very night. If there was even the smallest rainsquall, she was afraid that the power lines would fall and she would be left alone in the dark. Time after time, Louis stayed away from the fun and stayed home with Mother. He remarked that the only time he felt free was when he went away to college.

And then Louis married and he and Virginia had a child. Virginia immediately became a stand-in for his hovering, smothering, emotionally blackmailing mother. True, Virginia became increasingly suspicious of him, but I began to see that it was always with cause. And so, Louis wanted out of the marriage. It was difficult for him to accept, but after a time, when I felt that we had established enough of a rapport, I suggested that the issue was not whether or not the marriage survived, but rather that he resolve this feeling of being smothered. I even pointed out that he might go through a series of failed marriages, repeatedly feeling overwhelmed and wanting out.

Louis didn't argue. But it was clear from his posture, his silences, and even more from his actions, that he didn't agree. He began going through periods of missing sessions and/or canceling them at the last minute. He always had some reason: A client in Asia needed a promotion plan drawn up immediately, and he had to fly there to bring it to him. His boss needed him to do a high-tech presentation that no one else had the skills to do. At least twice, he stopped therapy because he didn't know when he would return from a trip to the Far East—could be weeks, he said. And then, after some weeks, he would again call to schedule an appointment. He was always apologetic. But ... but ... but he wasn't showing up.

Louis knew that Virginia wanted him to come to his sessions and would, in fact, check with him as to whether or not he was coming.

He sought revenge by failing to come to sessions, a form of acting out against the smothering approach he felt from his wife. But that was not all. He also felt smothered and choked by feeling he had to keep appointments with me. When difficult material came to the surface, exposed in his dreams, he would miss sessions.

I explained to him that he was doing the same thing in therapy that he was doing at home. "Your father ran out on you and your mother, and you feel compelled to do the same thing. If you want to divorce Virginia after you resolve this compulsion to leave, that's up to you. But then I would hope you leave, not because you were compelled to, but because you really wanted to. However, at present, the drive to leave and the need to sabotage this marriage is too intense."

Louis scowled. But I began to feel that he was listening.

It has been said that the main instrument for curbing the patient's compulsion to repeat and for turning it into a motive for remembering lies in the handling of the transference. We render the compulsion harmless, and indeed useful, by giving it the right to assert itself in a definite field. And in this field, Louis and I were tentatively moving forward. Louis had a series of dreams and recollections not only about his father's abandonment, but also about his father's outbursts toward him and his mother prior to leaving. He recalled the degrading and hurtful insults his father cast upon him and his mother and how hurt he was.

And yet, Louis had never seen or felt a connection between his feelings and urges toward Virginia and the hurtful behavior of his father. Nor had he made the connection about his reactions to Virginia, and his anger toward his dominating, suffocating mother. It was all there to be seen. It took a very long time.

Gradually, however, Louis began to change. The course of therapy was long and difficult. There were times when Louis continued to feel strangled—both by me and by his wife. But by recognizing what was happening, what he was causing to happen—and why—he began to see things for what they were. He no longer had to provoke problems with his wife. He was dealing with Virginia—not his mother. He no longer had to test out his freedom to come and go. He was dealing with Virginia, not his abandoning father. And for Virginia, though she had trouble trusting him, they both realized that it would take some time for the wounds to heal.

This marriage came close to ending. There was a prolonged separation, divorce attorneys were engaged, but Louis now wanted to try to work things out. He could talk things over when he felt his wife was checking up on him for no reason. He stopped missing sessions no matter how busy he was.

Louis came home every night and found pleasure in spending more time with his wife and son. When tensions arose, he was able to say, "Six months ago, if this disagreement between us occurred, I know what I would have done. I would have lost my temper, stormed out in a rage, and spent the night at a hotel feeling totally justified in what I was doing. I realize now that that is not the way to deal with arguments."

Change of this nature comes slowly, but as Louis began to own his role in many of the marital difficulties, he no longer had to reenact the trauma of his father's abandonment. He no longer felt the need to run away from difficulties.

As was said before, repeating early traumatic experiences is based upon acting them out through overt behavior rather than remembering the trauma and the feelings that accompanied the trauma. The more Louis was able to remember the pain of abandonment and degradation by his father, the less need there was to repeat it in his adult life.

Chapter 3

Repetitions in Child Rearing

It is hardly news that healthy parenting is vital for creating emotionally healthy children. Yet healthy parenting is not only difficult to achieve but sometimes even difficult to define. What's healthy? What's good for children? There are so many parenting styles. So which ones are good and which harmful?

Some parents come from backgrounds that were judgmental and harsh. Some come from parenting that was empathic and understanding. Both types of parents undoubtedly were formed by their own parents. So, can both kinds of parents become healthy parents themselves?

So much goes into answering that question. Parents can differ tremendously in their capacity to view their children as individuals who are growing into adults. Some can view behavior in their children as part of experimentation in the process of growth. This open and laissez-faire approach can be based upon a wish to see the children become independent and self-reliant adults. Such parents know that the children will make mistakes, and they accept that, viewing it as a learning process, so children can be prepared to make their own decisions. And sometimes, in a not so healthy way, these same parents can be reluctant to set limits for fear of stifling their children's spontaneity and imagination.

Other parents need to oversee every minute action of their children, to make certain that they learn "the right way to do things." They believe that it is their duty to inculcate their children with standards and values that are similar to their own. Sometimes, they demand total conformity from their children, down to the way they part their hair or brush their teeth. Their homes are run efficiently and possibly compulsively. Life, they believe, is filled with duties and requirements. If you turn on lights, then you must turn them off; if you sleep in your bed, then you must make it when you get up, etc.

Rather than view these scenarios as right or wrong, good or bad, it's important to view them as a reflection of the way the parents grew up and their beliefs. Both can work, though one is, I believe, infinitely more accommodating to the nature of children than the other. Both ways can work toward the health of the child if consistent messages are communicated. It is inconsistency that causes confusion and encourages manipulation and deviousness. Do mother and father agree on standards? Do they communicate similar messages to the children? Are they in agreement, and do they present their children with a united front? If so, all can be well and good.

If, on the other hand, children are exposed to the parents' own insecurities, doubts, and confusions, then one can almost guarantee that the children will inherit some of those insecurities. If there are unresolved conflicts that each parent had with his or her parents and which are being reenacted with the children, that especially is a recipe for trouble.

Marty was twelve years old the first time I met him, a very bright seventh grader, who had been coerced by his parents ("forced" might be a better word) to endure some sessions with me. It seemed that his entire life, friends, school, attitude, all was in flux, a mad roller coaster ride. For weeks, months even, he would do homework and school work devotedly and seriously, and he attained high grades. His friends were mostly mainstream kids, high-achieving and well-directed kids. At other times, Marty failed his classes. He became belligerent and negative. He dropped his mainstream friends and associated with kids on the fringe, kids on drugs, trouble makers. After a few weeks of this, he would again begin to study, to be self-directed into the kinds of good things he was capable of achieving, hanging around with his old, good friends—only to again begin a downward spiral.

His frantic parents had tried everything they knew to keep him on track or to get him back on track. They tried school counselors; they tried tutors. They tried medications—which Marty now refused to take. They had taken Marty to several other therapists before coming to me. Nothing seemed to hold for long however, and by the time they brought him to me, Marty had completely halted the roller coaster behavior, and was now simply headed down, down in a serious spiral.

I had met with his parents and learned of all this, and also learned how belligerent Marty had become. Also, since he had been to several other therapists, I knew that if I agreed to see Marty, I was up against a formidable foe, one who had obviously defeated all previous efforts to help him. What could I provide that no others had been able to provide? Certainly, I didn't consider myself infinitely more talented and wise than other professionals in this field. But I did have a certain degree of expertise here, and a whole lot of experience, and I believed I brought some empathy to this work. And here was a kid in need. I would do my best.

When the time came to meet with Marty, however, as prepared as I thought I was, I was quite unprepared for the depth of his anger. It was a winter afternoon when we met in my office, without his parents, just the two of us. He plopped into his chair across from me, crossed his arms and legs, and scowled at me.

"I don't want to be here," he said. "I don't need to be here. I've had it with 'experts' and you stupid shrinks. All anybody cares about is my grades, my friends. It's my life! So leave me alone! That's all I have to say to you. I'm not saying anything more. And if my parents want to waste their money, I can just sit here and waste it." Well, in some cases, as has been noted, silence can be an important psychotherapeutic tool. But clearly not in this case, and certainly not yet. And so, I quickly assured him that I didn't want him to come for therapy if he didn't want to. I also told him that I didn't much care about his grades or school achievements or any of the other things his parents were worried about.

"Ha!" he replied. And he rolled his eyes. "Then what am I here for?"

Ordinarily, that would have been a perfect opportunity to ask what *he* felt he was here for—or what he hoped to attain. But with Marty, there was no time for such quiet reflection, not yet. And so I went on to say that the only thing I did care about at this moment was that he felt pushed around by all these "experts." (Okay, in my head, I said, these *stupid shrinks*.) I added that I didn't want to be just one more of them. And I meant just that.

No answer.

Could he tell me more about his comment, "Why don't they leave me alone?"

Oh, yes, he had plenty to say about that. And so he began to talk, angrily. And I listened. As I did, as I learned about Marty's world, I again thought, as I have so often, that children have an uncanny ability to sense, and to act out, the unconscious of the parent. Sensitivities, doubts, feelings of inferiority, conflicts, all of these begin to be communicated to the child from the very first moment that the child enters his world. These clues are communicated as much by what is *un*said as by what is said, as much by what is *not* done, as by what is done. And, whoever we are in our innermost selves is communicated to the child. It forms and informs that child's character and development. It creates the child's very sense of *self*.

Some parents count on their children to bolster their own standing in their community. Their insecurities and fears of not being respected are imposed upon the child—who must then provide them with the status they desperately need. They live vicariously through their children. Such parents may place a high premium on achievement. The question at the dinner table is not "How are you feeling? What did you do today? Are you happy with your friends or teachers?" but rather, "Did you do your homework? Did you practice the piano? Did you win the game? Did you ace the test?"

The child is left with the inner question: Am I loved for me or am I loved for what I achieve?

And so I began to learn about Marty's family. I already knew, having met with his parents, that his father, Ben, was a physician, his mother, a schoolteacher. They were active in the community and had a wide circle of friends. Even to me, they had spoken about their many community activities and their friends' children. The father talked about other doctors and their families.

And this is what Marty brought up. "All they talk about is what they *do*, what their friends *do*," Marty said. "They bug me about my school work. They bug me to join this group. They want me to play on this team. I don't want to do those things. So they take me to shrinks, school counselors, tutors. And know what? All those 'experts' want is for me to do what my *parents* want me to do. They tell me how great my parents are. They tell me how smart I am. Yeah? Well, I don't want to hear it anymore."

I don't blame you, I thought.

I said, "I guess you feel no one really cares about what *you* want. You want to be who you are."

"Right," Marty growled.

Well. And how was I going to get that across to his obviously well meaning parents? They knew that Marty was at risk. He was on the cusp of a downward spiral, which could be repeated throughout his life. Marty wanted to be valued for himself, not for what he achieved. He didn't want to follow in his parents' footsteps. He wanted to be himself. And he couldn't be—couldn't even try to find out who he really was—because of parents who imposed their expectations on him.

His parents weren't evil. They had expectations. So what's wrong with that? Nothing. But there was something wrong here. It was that Marty's parents' expectations didn't take into account who Marty was—or even who he might want to become. They wanted achievements.

Marty wanted love.

It's what we all want.

And so, along with my sessions with Marty, I began a short series of sessions with Marty's parents, Ben and Andrea. For years, the common wisdom has been that children, and especially adolescents, should be seen alone in therapy with little contact with the parents. However, depending on the circumstances, I have found that there is much to be said for the same therapist working with the child and the parents.[1] Material can emerge, family dynamics uncovered, that often cannot be learned from the child alone. What was revealed to me in individual session with Ben, Marty's father, was that as a physician, he was kind and caring with his patients. He was renowned for that in the community, and also known as a clever diagnostician. He was one of those rare doctors who have plenty of time for patients, one who truly listens. His patients adored him. At home, however, even by his own admission, Ben was totally different. His insecurities were at rest at work—after all, as a physician, he was in charge. But at home, on a more personal level, if he was challenged, he could not tolerate it. He admitted that he became a raving maniac when Marty sassed him back.

"I'm sending him away!" Ben said. "He belongs in a military school. He'll soon shape up that way."

Now, the task of good therapy lies in the therapist helping the patient talk about, or more important, hear *himself* talk about his thoughts, feelings, memories. The empathic therapist, the creative therapist, is able to listen with a third ear, to articulate and interpret what the patient is really saying.

In this case, Ben wanted me to hear certain things—but I was beginning to hear something totally different. He wanted me to hear his complaints about his rebellious son. He had already made up his mind that Marty should be sent away to a boarding school—and he wanted me to agree. He felt that Marty should be punished or treated with "tough love." He wanted me to agree. He wanted me to agree with his ideas about what a son should and should not do.

What I felt he did not want was to discover that his rebellious son was only expressing unconsciously the father's own history. When we moved away from talking about Marty, I learned a lot about Ben. I learned that Ben was the firstborn son of parents who had told him almost from childhood that he would be an A student who would go on to medical school. It was what they demanded of him. He would become a source of pride to them. Over and over, this was drilled into him. He, the firstborn, would be "Our son. The doctor."

Ben, however, while adept and clever at his medical and premed studies, loved music. He was a talented violinist. He not only performed the repertoire of written musical scores with grace and talent, but he also composed his own music, complete with scores for the orchestra. His friends and his community in school and college were also musicians. They were his life, his source of fulfillment.

His parents endured this. They humored him. They agreed that his musical interests and aspirations were fine—for a hobby. But—*you can't make a decent living as a musician. You will become a doctor.*

And so he did. He became a doctor and a good one. He gave up his music. So how did this relate to Marty? I thought I knew. But I knew, too, that this was going to be a hard thing for Ben to hear. I wondered if he would rail in anger at me—as he clearly did at his son—when hearing things he did not want to hear. And so I proceeded slowly. I had already gotten hints that he had some anger at me and some at the other "quack therapists who weren't even medical doctors," the therapists to whom they had taken Marty before. He felt they had fed him nonsense. So why should he not think the same of me? We worked together for some months, and I began to see that if he didn't completely agree with me on certain issues, he certainly had become more willing to listen. Finally, when I felt we had established a therapeutic alliance, a comfort zone, I brought up the material that I thought I knew.

"I hear in your behavior toward your son," I said, "that a part of you is screaming to be free, to be the person you wanted to be. I hear your resentment at the fact that you had to give up your dream. You've abandoned your music. You miss it."

For a moment, he simply stared at me. He opened and closed his mouth. He said not a word, but he looked—stunned? Angry? Had I spoken too soon? Had I provoked him before he was ready? And then he swallowed and breathed deeply, and I saw that tears were forming in his eyes.

I went on, gently, "Maybe you're angry at your son because he's rebelling in a way that you could not?"

He bent his head and broke down in tears.

It was a beginning. It was a good beginning. But it was only the beginning. Next came the hard work, because though insights are important, vital to good therapy, insights without changes in behavior are worse than useless. Could Ben now change his relationship with Marty following this realization? Could he empathize with what his son was going through? Could he admire his son for his attempts to do what he, Ben, had been unable to do? Or was he going to continue to try and pummel Marty into submission, as had happened to him?

It was a long, tumultuous time with Marty, with Ben, with them both. But Marty's downward spiral was stopped. And eventually, surprisingly to Marty, he began to achieve just the kinds of things his parents had hoped for. And many things that they had not. Most surprising of all, perhaps, eventually, this was all right with Marty's father.

The setting of limits and degrees of freedom are more a reflection of the parents' own experiences as children themselves. Because there is a legitimate question here: Don't children need limits? Do they not feel more secure knowing that even freedom has boundaries? How and to what degree should boundaries be set? As we have seen, children are sometimes inadvertently used by the parent to express what is unknown to the parent. We spoke of children's exquisite sensitivities and how children are often the vicarious spokespersons for one parent or the other. This may sound rather spooky, but it is striking how often a child behaves or says things much to the chagrin of the parent that hits close to the core of their lives.

There is another aspect to the parent-child relationship that is often played out in marital relationships. The child needs to be protected and cared for; the child needs the parent. The parent needs the child. In most close relationships there is a state of ambivalence. Parents can desire to protect their children, but it is inconvenient and, at times, a downright pain. Children interfere with parental activities and with their freedom. They are demanding and parents may resent this. Similarly, children need their parents, but as they grow, they need to feel free and independent, at times to the dismay of parents who may try to interfere with their efforts to be independent. Unless there is an ability to accept ambivalence in the relationship—the parent's wish to be free of the child or the child's wish to be free of the parent—there can be mixed and contradictory messages communicated from one to the other. The mother who has a need to see herself as all-giving and deserving of appreciation or the child who feels guilty for wanting to assert some independence is the cause of conflict. There are strings attached to the giving translated as—*After all I've done for you, after all I sacrificed, how could you treat me like this?* The stage is set for emotional blackmail. In this formulation love is not given, it's owed. Independence is not a child's right as part of development. Rather, it is seen as ungrateful rejection.

Nor is it always or even most often the parents' conscious or intentional behavior that has the greatest impact on the growth and development of children. Rather, it is the unconscious repressed needs and impulses of the parents that find vicarious gratification in children and especially in adolescents. The child acts out the forbidden desires and receives unconscious encouragement for troublesome and unacceptable behavior that the parents and society discourage. Thus the child receives mixed and inconsistent messages. While acting out behavior that is condoned unconsciously, he becomes confused, for he is being discouraged and even punished consciously.

In some cases, children get into trouble not because of any overt behavior, but because of their parents' fears and expectations of what their children will do. These expectations are often unexpressed but nevertheless communicated to the child. They represent feelings and impulses that the parents have inhibited in themselves. Unless parents become aware of and are able to accept such inner promptings in themselves, they will continue to place their children in a contradictory double bind.[2]

Such was the case with Zach. A cute, bright, lively six-year-old, Zach was an embarrassment to his mother. At home, he was well behaved and generally did as he was told. School was quite a different story. He was a cut-up in the first grade, the class clown, and the class trouble maker. His parents, Jared and Cookie Whitfield, were called into school repeatedly to be told about Zach's behavior.

Now, it is not unusual for children who misbehave in school to be upset about things at home—yet home seemed great. The Whitfields lived in a large beautiful home in the right kind of town with all the right accoutrements—swimming pool, Jacuzzi, gym, den, large-screen TV, etc. The father, Jared, came from a family of money and he, in turn, earned lots of money. He wasn't home much because he worked long hours, but when he was home, he was very popular at the Country Club, had many friends, and played tennis and golf. I learned that Jared went to boarding school when he turned eleven. That's what happened with his father, his uncles, and his grandfather.

Similarly, Cookie left home for "finishing school" when she was twelve, had her "coming-out party" at seventeen, and was now socially connected and very active in charitable events. She chaired many activities and was busy with friends and relatives.

Zach and his little sister were growing up with nannies and au pairs, most of whom were good at caring for them both. Zach went to a private Country Day school although the public schools in their elite town were among the best. They took summer and winter vacations together. Why would Zach be so difficult at school? No one had the answer, but the school could not continue to tolerate his disruptive behavior. Admonitions didn't help; prohibitions and punishments didn't help. In desperation, the Whitfields decided to try psychotherapy.

During play with me, Zach was much taken with toy soldiers and knights and ogres. He set up elaborate battles that resulted in much bloodshed and, of course, my side always lost. It seemed to me that Zach was angry, though he never said he was angry. The only anger he expressed was a rather normal one, the main culprit being his little sister.

One day when he came in, he told me he had fallen off his bike the day before. He showed me the scrape. It was an ugly thing, one of the road burn scrapes, red and angry looking.

I frowned and said that it must have hurt. He sighed. "It does. A little." "But," he added, "All kids fall off their bikes and get hurt."

"Is that so?" I asked.
He nodded. "Uh, huh."
"But it must have hurt a lot. Did you cry?"
He shrugged and shook his head. "You shouldn't cry."
"Really?" I asked. "Even if it hurts?"
He nodded. "Somebody told you that?" I asked.
"My Mom."

And though I tried to provoke him into talking about that statement, he seemed to feel that was the end of the conversation. His mother told him to stop crying because all kids fall off bikes and scrape themselves and that was the end of it.

Christmas vacation was coming and the family went away together for two weeks. Following his return, Zach seemed more calm and less anxious to fight play battles. He chattered and seemed quite a normal, relaxed little kid.

I remarked that he seemed much happier now than when he was in school. He said no. He liked school. And so, I wondered out loud, why he thought he might be feeling happier that day. He said that he felt happy because he'd been with his parents. He liked having them around.

"But they're always around," I said. "Even when you're at school, your mom's at home and your dad's at work."

"No," he shot back. "They're always out."

"And you like them to be home?"

"Well, *some* of the time," Zach answered.

I asked Zach if he could tell his mom that he liked her to be home sometimes. He said no. He couldn't. "She'll get upset," he said sadly.

"Mad?" I questioned.

He shook his head. "No. Just upset."

"You're sure?"

"Uh, huh." He nodded.

Herein lay the key, I felt sure. The clear message in the Whitfield household was this: Don't talk about unpleasant feelings. When Zach had hurt himself in his fall from his bike, he came home crying. *Boys don't cry*, said his mother.

A short while after this, I had a session with Zach's parents, starting first with his dad, Jared, in a one-on-one conversation. I asked him how he had felt when he left home to go to boarding school at eleven.

He shrugged. "I don't know. That's the way it was in the family. When you turn eleven, you go to boarding school."

"Yes," I persisted. "But how did you feel about it?"

Again, he shrugged. Again he repeated that he was simply following the family traditions.

Again, I said, "But how did you feel about it?"

Feel? It seemed to be a foreign word to him. After a time of being quiet, Jared finally admitted to being scared. He hadn't wanted to leave home and he said he'd been terribly homesick. He remembered telling his parents that—just once. They told him that he'd get over it. Jared finally admitted that he was terribly angry with his parents for sending him away to school. He felt they wanted to get rid of him and he had urges to run away from the boarding school knowing that this would upset his parents.

Next session, I met with Cookie. I asked about her going to finishing school and got a similar go-round. *Feel?* What did that have to do with it? It was only in a later session that Cookie told me that during college she went through a period of terrible loneliness and depression. She had seen a counselor there for a few sessions, though she had told no one about it.

It seemed clear to me that the Whitfields did not permit their feelings to get in the way of what had to be done. Feelings were forbidden. Emotional expression was forbidden, whether in words or in action. No words. No tantrums. No tears. Big boys don't cry. (Girls don't see therapists, either.)

It took some doing to communicate to Jared and Cookie that Zach was doing them a favor. By his behavior, he was crying out for more attention, more of their time, more closeness. He wanted and needed to have his feelings heard. He didn't want to stoically accept things the way they were as his parents had done—and, in fact, were still doing. They both admitted that they were so caught up in being busy that they had little time to deal with feelings they had for each other or for the children. They also admitted that they were moving farther apart and that they rarely really shared feelings openly between them. They did what they had to do. That was the motto of their families of origin. They were simply passing this onto their kids.

Cookie saw Jared as being distant emotionally, but she did not disagree when I suggested that distancing seemed to be something they both did in their relationship to their parents, to each other, and to their children.

But, they both loved their kids. They loved one another, in the emotionally distant way they had of relating. And, most important, after seeing what was happening, they were willing to change. Jared made an effort to be home more and to spend more time with Zach.

Cookie tried to reduce her commitments outside the family. Both parents became more responsive to their own feelings and even their disappointments and frustrations with each other. They especially began to be more sensitive to the feelings that lay behind Zach's behavior. Zach gradually was better able to express his feelings at home and—no surprise at all!—his behavior at school improved.

CHILDREN OF DIVORCE

The belief and expectation on the part of all children is that their parents will live together in harmony. Whether the family is the traditional father-and-mother family, whether it is a two-father family or two-mother family, or whether it is a single-mother family, all children want the same thing. They want, and need, and deserve, to be embraced within the shelter of a family, whatever form that family might take. And yet—things happen. Death happens. Wars and conflicts tear families apart and leave them separated, sometimes for years on end. Sometimes permanently. Divorce happens.

And divorce stinks, especially for children. Ask anyone who has ever been involved in a divorce, and especially ask a child, and that is what you will hear.

An important study was commissioned that followed children whose parents had divorced for twenty-five years. Those children were found to experience many more difficulties in love, intimacy, and commitment to their marriages than a control group whose parents had not divorced. In addition, the children of divorce had many more difficulties in their role as parents.[3]

Divorce is almost always the end point of years of dissension, expressed or unexpressed, between parents. There are parents who pride themselves on the fact that there was not much bickering prior to the divorce. "We never argue in front of the children," they tell me. But that is false, at least in the heart of the matter if not in actuality. Because kids know that dissension exists. Kids have an incredible radar for picking up on unspoken clues. (I sometimes think that kids would make superb therapists.)

Certainly, when there is much arguing and dissension prior to divorce, some children might say, "I can't stand it anymore, I wish they'd get it over with." And there is truth to that, for it is not good for children to be exposed to arguing and nitpicking by parents. It is also not easy to determine whether the children are better off with divorce or with perpetual disagreements. But either way, divorce is traumatic, just as growing up and living in a dysfunctional family is traumatic. Children are scarred either way. When the divorce happens, it is an emotional blow. Young children feel the loss even with joint custody and are left in a state of confusion. With adolescents, the parents often lose credibility in their children's eyes. The formulation becomes this: *Why should I pay any attention to you when you can't get your own act together? I'll make my own decisions and do what I want to do.* This is particularly true when one parent continually speaks badly of the other. This creates conflict for the child, and it places a burden on the child. If the child visits the father and, possibly, the father's partner, and likes them, she may feel guilty for betraying the mother who has been hurt and is furious with him. If the child feels a strong allegiance to the mother, he cannot allow himself to abandon the already abandoned mother. Some children feel that they must rescue the hurt parent, thus taking on a burden that is too much for them. If the parent continues to feel depressed despite the child's attempts to rescue, that child can feel that he or she is a failure.

Even worse, children sometimes believe that the divorce happened because they have not been good enough. In other words, it's all their fault. "If I would have been a better kid, if I would have behaved better, if I would not have got into trouble, then the divorce would not have happened." And this kind of belief persists despite being told by both parents that the child had nothing to do with the decision to divorce. And often children are misused on the battlefield between parents who are at war with each other. With divorce, children become caught in the battle between parents who war for their loyalty. This, of course, only serves to foster more conflict in the children.

Sandy was an engaging seven-year-old girl whose parents had divorced. Her dad, Gregory, had remarried and Greg's new wife, Elizabeth, though she had warm feelings toward Sandy, didn't like some of the ways Sandy was being raised by her mother. Greg was a passive man, and in marrying Elizabeth, he had married a woman not unlike his first wife, Sandy's mother. He sat back on the sidelines and the women ran the show. On one weekend when Sandy came to visit with her father, a mundane but volatile issue arose. Mother kept Sandy's hair on the long side, with sweet, low bangs that came down almost to her eyes. Her stepmother, Elizabeth, said Sandy looked like a messy sheepdog. She pressured Greg to take Sandy for a haircut. No, he couldn't. Sandy's mom didn't want it, had expressly instructed him not to have Sandy's hair cut. Despite this, Elizabeth dragged Sandy to a hairdresser. On Sunday night, when Dad brought Sandy back home to Mom, Mom was furious at the sight of Sandy's short hair. She raged. Greg was stumped by her anger. What was the big deal? It was only a haircut.

Or was it?

The whole scenario sounds stupid. It was stupid. But it happened and it happens in many families. And what was the result? The result was that after this scene—and many others like it—Sandy didn't want to visit her father and Elizabeth anymore. It just caused fights. Her dad, her mom, her stepmom, they all got angry. She didn't want to be part of it. She cowered when told it was time to go see her dad. She refused to go. Greg, of course, became furious with his ex-wife for not upholding the visitation agreements. He ordered her back to court.

Did this belong in the courts? No. But could any of them, except perhaps for Sandy, recognize it? Again, no.

So what was the result? Stepmother, Elizabeth, succeeded in separating her husband from his daughter. Greg's passivity caused more trouble and anger between him and his former wife. There was also trouble now between Greg and his new wife, Elizabeth. And Sandy, a little seven-year-old, was caught up in the mess. Worse, she began to feel that it was all her fault.

The self-sabotage occurred on all levels and with all parties. Father repeated with his new wife the same issues that occurred in his first marriage with Sandy's mother. He was passive and tried to please everyone because when he grew up, he felt he had to be his mother's "good boy" because his father left her. He was unable to assert himself with Sandy's mother, which contributed to the divorce. He was unable to assert himself with his second wife, which created the strained situation when she undermined his relationship with his daughter. Sandy's mother was opinionated and open about her feelings. Sandy's stepmother was domineering and divisive and Greg could not stand up to her. Every adult contributed to sabotaging the relationship. But a seven-year-old was the victim. One has to wonder: Because of her confusion and self-recrimination, will she too grow up to become a self-sabotaging adult?

One can only hope not.

And I think: We have to do better than that.

Chapter 4

Penitential Repetitions: Repetitions of Rescue and Repentance

Most small children start out believing that the world revolves around them. This is a normal stage of development, infantile feelings of grandiosity and narcissism, a sense that one is the center of the universe. With normal development, that feeling gradually recedes. However, when certain parents place the children in the middle of their own lives and also their conflicts, this normal process can be interrupted. The result is that many of these children develop a severe sense of responsibility, guilt, and self-recrimination. They are left with a harsh and punitive conscience, self-doubts, and lack of confidence. If anything goes wrong with either parent or with the family, they believe it is not only their fault, but that it is their responsibility to right the wrongs or to repair the damage. This attitude extends beyond the family to a generalized feeling that their role in life is to correct, to help, to set things right. And if they cannot set things right (and what child can rescue an alcoholic parent, for example?) the child grows up believing that she or he has failed. And thus the stage is set for the grownup child to continue to try and fix the world.

The view of one's self as the rescuer becomes part of the way one deals with others. The child who feels compelled to make life better for an abused parent becomes the adult who must make life better for others, even at his own expense. There develops an attraction to others who are needy and the rescuer comes to the rescue. He or she marries someone who appears to be helpless or weak or incompetent. The individual takes over and, of course, achieves rewards for being so helpful, so wonderful. However, the deeper motives may not really be so charitable. What begins out of pity and concern for the bereft parent, who may have been abandoned, becomes a way of life, a need to do for others while denying one's own needs. Eventually, the individual feels used up and exhausted because all the energy is going out and not enough support is coming in. When one feels depleted and taken advantage of, one is likely to feel angry.

Norman was a forty-nine-year-old thrice-married successful entrepreneur who announced that he collected "wounded birds." The wounded birds were his ex-wives, all of whom Norman recognized belatedly to be not what they had seemed. Prior to marrying these women, Norman found them to be beautiful, loving, intelligent, and, he thought, independent. It turned out that they were beautiful and intelligent, but not loving and not at all independent. Instead, they were demanding, manipulative, and exceedingly dependent. Everything was fine as long as these women got what they wanted. And they all knew exactly what they wanted—and they wanted a lot. This third wife in particular was adamant and relentless. Her demands were often totally unreasonable. Yet if Norman didn't agree, he was met with a barrage of rationalizations and justifications and outbursts of fury. From the choice of the location of a table at a restaurant to the choice of friends, to the choice of vacations, there were good reasons behind everything. And if Norman resisted even a little, then came the cajoling, the seducing, the manipulation. Suddenly, the certain, demanding woman would become the weak, fearful, sick person who could not be refused. She was entitled to what she wanted and it was up to Norman to supply it.

This third wife did not have a job or a career although she was well educated and could have gotten any number of well-paying jobs had she wished. (The same had been true of wife number one and two.) Also, she could not possibly take care of the chores around the house. She needed a laundress, a cleaning service, etc. She needed, in fact, everything: clothes, jewels, vacations.

Norman really, really wanted to please her. He wanted to please all women. He wanted to see them happy and satisfied. He would try to gratify their wishes until he realized that they went on and on. The enormous bills came in each month. But questioning the expenditures on new clothes, jewelry, hairdressers were not up for discussion. "You just don't understand what things cost. You don't understand women. You don't care how I look. I would be the laughing stock if I wore that dress again." Or, "How could you even think of going there on vacation? You know I have all these allergies and how sick I get. We have to go somewhere that will not irritate my allergies." These were the answers and there was no room for negotiation.

So why did Norman find himself in that situation over and over again? He needed to bolster his self-esteem by demonstrating that he could please and satisfy beautiful women, and he chose women who demanded that they be pleased. He needed women who feigned helplessness so that he could be the rescuer. He didn't want his wives to work since that would undermine his position as the giver, the savior. Though he complained about it, Norman needed to be the sugar daddy to the cute and demanding little girl—until he could not satisfy her any longer. He needed women who needed to be rescued. And he tried, but was left feeling that his efforts were never enough. His needs to feel important to save others were met with feelings of failure because the bar was constantly being raised.

As we worked together, I discovered that Norman's father had been brutal. He was verbally abusive to the family and he barely eked out a living. He was critical and chronically discontented. Norman's mother felt she had no choice but to stay with her husband. There was not enough money and she had three young children. Norman felt that he had to console, support, and make life better for his mother who would confide in him about her unhappy lot in life. Norman felt sorry for his mother and vowed early that he would not treat women the way his father did and that he would never turn out to be the man his father was. In fact, Norman spent much of his life trying *not* to be like his father.

Norman had excelled in school, and through work and scholarships, he completed college majoring in business. He wanted to make money to escape the poverty he grew up in and to give money to his mother to make life better and easier for her. He did very well and extended his needs to rescuing other women. Of course, he also needed rescuing by reassuring himself that he was a success, which was measured not only by his earning power, but also by being able to aggrandize himself by being with beautiful, attractive women who needed him. However, by the time he came to me, he recognized that he had gotten more than he bargained for.

Norman was fearful of repeating this pattern that he recognized, but felt helpless to stop. He could not say no to any woman, and especially not to this wife. She would not only cajole when he could not satisfy her, she became infuriated with him, degrading him and actually emptying out his clothes and throwing them all around the house. She became increasingly demanding and abusive and he kept coming back for more. He could not leave her, could not bring himself to leave her.

It was hard work for Norman to eventually see what was happening—and why. He finally came to the epiphany that he was paying penance for his guilty rage at his father. Though he received satisfaction by pleasing his mother, this was purchased at the expense of treating his father as a nonperson and he had guilty anger at doing for his mother what his father could not do. He won his mother's affection at the expense of his father.

He could not leave this wife precisely because she was most abusive and satisfied his needs to be punished. He needed to please and to be punished at the same time and she filled the bill. Norman's resolution to this dilemma was to leave his third wife, and to offer her a settlement that was far more generous than was necessary or even agreed upon by his attorney. Norman had to pay his dues in spades.

He broke down in tears when he heard himself say that he never had a father he could admire, that he never had a childhood, and that he assumed responsibilities for his mother when he should have been free to be a child. He was sad and he was angry. He felt relief, like a burden was removed when he experienced and expressed his pained feelings about going it alone and having no one really to support him in the process of growing up to be a man. His conception that manliness meant deferring to and fulfilling the wishes and expectations of women was erroneous. He was seeking confirmation of himself by saving "wounded birds" and that was not what he really wanted. He cried when he realized that he had needs to be taken care of, that he had been deprived of the caring and pride of having a father who appreciated his son and wanted the best for him. He was angry that he did not have this. He was angry that he had to be his mother's caregiver and that he was cared for only for what he did in being the caregiver of his mother. He felt cheated and deprived. "Why did I have to be the husband or the father and never the child or the son? I chose women who would demand of me so that I could continue to bury my own needs in order to take care of them when I really needed someone to give to me, to take care of me." He recalled a few occasions when his former wife would try to offer him solace and support. He rejected it in anger. He avoided facing his own deep-seated dependency needs feeling he was being demeaned as a man. "I couldn't let them give to me. I had to be the big shot because I couldn't bear to accept my own needs to be a child who had needs."

I don't know what happened to Norman after he terminated therapy, but I do know that when he left, he felt more whole. He was a human being who could acknowledge that he no longer needed to save "wounded birds," simply because he himself had been wounded.

Laura came to therapy because she was ready to divorce her husband. "I can't take his drinking any longer," she said. "He refuses to stop. He refuses to go to AA. He insists that he is not an alcoholic and insists that he doesn't have a drinking problem."

I take a history, usually at the first session, asking for details about parents and siblings in order to develop a context in which to place the patient and his/her situation.

"My father was basically a good and kind person with a good sense of humor except for the times that he drank," Laura said. "When he did drink, he was distant, withdrawn, and gave us all the silent treatment. The family learned to leave him alone then. We grew up feeling that this was the way things had to be. But I resented it. He was so great one day and so absent the next day. I could not tolerate his inconsistency and his unpredictability the way my mother did. I swore to myself that I would not and could not live that way. And I cannot. And I will not."

When I asked Laura about her husband, she said he was a hard worker and a good provider. The children loved him. "But he drinks and I won't live with it."

Now, it is extremely important for therapists to be alert to the impact of alcohol on patients and their families. Though individuals may not get drunk or lose time at work, some people with even one drink experience a change in their personalities, a change in the way they relate to others. In other words, it is not the amount or the frequency of drinking that defines the alcoholic. Rather it is what alcohol does to the person and his relationships. I wondered about the effect of drinking on Laura's husband's behavior.

"He doesn't get drunk, he doesn't miss work, he's good around the house, but he has wine with dinner every night!"

Could Laura be overreacting based upon her traumatic childhood experiences with her own father? It seemed possible. But caution was necessary here before I came to such a conclusion. I then asked to meet with her husband, who came willingly. He was at a loss as to understand why Laura was ready to seek a divorce.

"I don't see why I should give up a glass or two of wine with dinner. I enjoy it. It relaxes me and that's as far as it goes. It does not affect my chores, my relationship with my kids, or my functioning on my job. It wouldn't affect the way I feel with my wife, but that she makes such a big deal about it. It's not the glass of wine that's causing the problem. It's Laura. She's driving me crazy. She wants me to go to AA. I have nothing against AA. I know that a lot of alcoholics deny that they have problems with alcohol. But I really don't. There is no alcoholism in my family. The most I have is two glasses of wine with dinner and I never drink otherwise and the wine doesn't do anything else to me. I never drink too much or get drunk. It just doesn't make sense to me."

It didn't make sense. To him. But it did make sense to Laura. It made a kind of inner sense, because Laura was reacting, not to what was today but to what was a very long time ago. She was reacting to her father. She was expecting a problem with alcohol and she was creating a problem that wasn't there, based upon fear.

This was discussed with Laura who had a hard time accepting the fact that she was overreacting. She could not believe that she had been so traumatized by her father's drinking that she had become hypersensitive to this degree—a common reaction to any trauma. Laura was repeating her past. She felt she had failed in her efforts to get her father to stop drinking resulting in the fact that her primary family was dysfunctional. She believed that it was her responsibility to stop her father's drinking and she failed. Now she had to stop her husband from doing what her father had done. She could not fail again! She was sticking by her vow not to live with a drinker. But she was still repeating her past in ways that were endangering her marriage. It took intervention and insight and much time for Laura to see that she could be married to—even would *like* to be married to—a man who had a glass of wine at dinner. She was trying to rescue her husband, who, in fact, had no need of being rescued.

There is a belief, common to so many, that permeates much of our thinking and it is this: The thought equals the act. Forbidden wishes and fantasies are experienced as the same as actions. We feel as guilty for what we think, wish for, or fantasize as we would feel had we done it. In other words, the young child who wishes his parents would die because they don't give him what he wants must beg forgiveness, not for what he's done but for what he's thought. The jealous wife acts as if her husband is unfaithful to her if he so much as looks at other women—because of this deep-seated belief that the *thought* equals the *act*.

Psychologically, human beings, children as well as adults, are capable of all kinds of wishes, thoughts, and fantasies. They are part of the human condition; they are what keeps the child alive within us as adults; they are necessary for creativity. They are to be celebrated rather than erased. Yet many people spend their lives paying penance for what they have thought and not for what they have done. Survivors want to survive their horrible ordeals. The urge is to preserve life, preserve the species. Yet, if a person survives when those around him do not, he can feel guilty, guilty because his wish to survive became a reality that is experienced as being at the expense of those who perished. It is assumed that this is an instance of "Schadenfreude," joy in seeing others suffer, though that is not the case.

When Lynne first came to me, I found her to be bright, highly motivated to achieve, and driven, a workaholic in fact. She assumed responsibilities above and beyond what was necessary both on the job and in volunteer work. She was always overwhelmed. But she also received kudos for what she did—she got promotions, she won awards, she got recognition. She took on more than she could handle and it got the better of her. I learned that after college she had made her first suicide attempt, ending up in the hospital. She was discharged to outpatient treatment with a therapist with whom she was able to relate. But the contract was made clear. If she attempted suicide again without giving the therapist advanced notice, the therapy would stop. Lynne got a new and more demanding job. She undertook graduate studies. She became more active in more organizations. She continued in therapy. She became overwhelmed and attempted suicide again. The therapist dismissed her. It was following this second hospitalization that Lynne was referred to me.

Lynne was motivated to work out her problem, but it was a tough problem. One of the first things I learned was that early in Lynne's adolescence, Lynne's mother had committed suicide. No one knew why this happened. Lynne and her mother had gotten on well and the loss of her mother was cause for Lynne's confusion, sadness, and loneliness. Lynne had no one to talk to. Her mother's suicide was a shock and in this state of shock, Lynne could not feel. She was angry, but could not allow herself to feel anger at her mother. She was sad, but could not allow herself to mourn her mother's death. All she knew was that she was alone. She just plodded along the best she could, doing well in high school and college. She was popular, active in organizations, a high achiever. She continued to be raised by her father who was and always had been remote and distant to both his wife and daughter. He went on with life as if little of significance happened following the suicide of his wife and his child's mother. He was a presence for Lynne, but that was about all. He demonstrated little empathy for what she experienced because he was so distant himself.

Lynne longed for and needed the caring that she lost when her mother committed suicide. "Why would she do something like that? Why would she leave me? What did I do to cause her to take her life?" Lynne wondered.

As Lynne and I worked together, we delved into her self-blame for her mother's suicide. We dealt with her anger at her mother for abandoning her, her father's remoteness. We discussed his second wife's horrible behavior toward Lynne. But most of all, we dealt with

Lynne's feelings. Most important, she felt that she must pay penance for letting her mother down. In what way? She did not know. But she knew she must have been somehow to blame. She had this awful, gnawing feeling that she had disappointed her mother in some terrible way. She gradually realized, however, that behind her compulsive, driven behavior was a drive to make her mother proud of her and to gain her mother's forgiveness. Forgiveness? Yes, because it was as if her mother's suicide was due to some wish on Lynne's part that she die and that when her mother committed suicide, it was Lynne's fault. Though she had no recollection of such a wish, chances are good that somewhere in the process of growing up, Lynne, like all other children, had death wishes toward her parents.

Lynne again began her compulsive overwhelming behavior and we called a halt to her tendency to assume so much. She began to understand that her flights into busyness represented her way of proving that she was worthwhile and valuable. It helped to compensate for her overwhelming belief that her mother committed suicide because of Lynne's imagined failures. The busyness also helped smother her repressed feelings of anger and loss—a loss that she had never mourned. Lynne was able to realize that she was putting herself under intense pressures to prove herself. She came to see and to feel that her mother's suicide had nothing to do with her and was motivated by reasons that Lynne might never know. But she realized that she was not the cause of it and that she did not have to kill herself through work or through suicide to pay penance.

This required a major change in lifestyle for her. When she felt tempted to assume more and more responsibilities, she talked this over. She felt a vacuum for not throwing herself into activities. She feared she was taking the easy way out by having leisure time, by enjoying herself. Lynne had to pay the ultimate price by dying herself through her own suicide attempts. When one suffers a loss like this and does not mourn, there is an internal price to be paid, most often in the form of depression. Lynne was depressed and angry and she wanted to either kill herself through suicide or through working herself to death.

Lynne did not want to die. She had a lust for life that she could not savor without feeling even more guilty. During the course of our work, she was able to express the anger, the disappointment, the pain of the death of her mother. She was able to go through a mourning period without throwing herself into frenetic activities. The vacuum she felt when she tried to force herself not to be overwhelmed with busyness dissipated so that finally, she was able to enjoy living without having to justify her existence to her mother. She could also allow herself to enjoy life without fleeing into compulsive activities.

I never want to be like my mother.

As a therapist, I hear this theme again and again. "I never want to be like my mother. When I was little, I promised myself that when I grew up, I would never be like that. But the older I become, the more I realize that I'm acting the same way she did."[1]

The internalization of these early relationships, as negative as they might be, is powerful and persistent. One might reject it in words, but it can live in the unconscious. It can ruin future relationships and ruin lives. And it occurs in insidious ways. There are times when an individual is filled with doubts about her own abilities. Perhaps she really doesn't feel capable and up to the responsibilities of a job. She asks for help, but when help is offered, she vents anger at the helper.

This process is repeated again and again. Instead of *killing the messenger*, it's a case of *killing the helper*.

Mark had been married to Sally for ten years. There were no children. Mark was well educated, but not a great earner. His resume was spotty. He worked here and there doing fairly well, only to repeatedly find himself out of a job.

Sally, on the other hand, had a long-standing responsible position. She got good annual performance reviews and bonuses and she earned a good salary. When she and Mark came to me, she presented herself as self-confident and independent. She was also angry. She was quick to point out that Mark wasn't contributing to the family in the way he should have and she felt that she had been let down.

What began to quickly emerge, however, was that Sally, despite her self-assured facade, was very insecure. In spite of what she professed on the surface, she did not really feel that she deserved the position she had. When she was given projects, she sometimes felt overwhelmed. It was then that she would turn to Mark to help, help in doing the research or the math that was required to solve technical problems with her project. Mark was willing to help, and quite capable, besides. He had many talents that were of use to her. And yet—though Sally had asked for his help—she resented it. She resented having to ask for it, and she resented receiving the help she asked for. She felt, although she had not yet acknowledged it to herself, that needing Mark demeaned her.

And where did that leave Mark? Mark felt he was in a no-win situation with her. He was getting contradictory messages from her. On the one hand, he was being asked to help. When he helped, she got angry. She was furious, in fact. She was militant in her need to be independent, to do it all herself. Yet when she couldn't do it herself, she felt weakened and vulnerable, asked for help, and ... yes, it was a vicious cycle. What was Mark to do? What was any individual to do in such a situation?

Sally told me early on: I never want to be like my mother. Her mother was angry being a woman. She was angry having a husband and children who needed her. In fact, her mother was always angry. Mother would give because she felt she had to, but she resented every moment of it. She gave, resented, and then withdrew from those who pulled at her. Though Sally clearly said, "I never want to be like my mother," she was behaving in the same way. She, like her mother, needed to preserve the image she had of being capable, of having no dependency needs herself, largely because exposing dependency meant getting hurt.

Mark became her mother who helped at her request, but Sally recreated the scenario in which *asking for help is followed by rejection*. Mark, in turn, had a need to keep helping and rescuing to compensate for his own feelings of inadequacy due to his failure to maintain jobs and to contribute equally to the family's finances (as well as by circumstances from his own past). By helping Sally, he was bolstering himself. Sally would not let him do that and this cycle repeated itself until Mark called a halt to it. Mark reached a point of being fed up with being the rescuer only to be demeaned and he wanted out of the relationship.

A word is in order about Sally's desire to be not like her mother. Sally was only dimly aware of this dynamic, but the more it became clearly articulated, the more she was able to interrupt her behavior that was destructive to her and her husband. As I pointed out to both Mark and Sally, they were at risk of repeating this interactive behavior whether it was in relation to this marriage or to future marriages.

By repeating, we believe we can master, but this too often leads to disaster. It seems as if there is an inexorable drive to undermine, to undo changes that are hard won. How dare I? How dare I have a good marriage when my mother suffered through her rotten marriage to my father? How dare I succeed in my work when my father hated his job? How dare I enjoy life when others close to me cannot? How dare I live when those close to me perished? My guilt deprives me of consolidating and celebrating my accomplishments and good fortune. My success must be undone.

Survivor guilt is powerful. It prevents people from succeeding in the first place or it leads to cycles of self-sabotage in which one succeeds and then must undermine the success by failing. Troubled marriages improve only to be upended by the destructive behavior of one or the other spouse and the trouble begins again. Alcoholics face their problem and stop drinking only to find themselves drinking again despite their vows that their drinking days are over once and for all. The good life, the peaceful life is intolerable. Survivors cannot tolerate peace and tranquility. They need agitation, they need trouble in order to feel alive.

"When I'm in the middle of a knockdown drag-out fight with my wife, I get a rush, a feeling of being alive," one man said to me. "I need to have tension. Without tension and without problems, I feel bored and dead."

This is a theme that recurs frequently, though not always obviously. The fighting, the tension, is rationalized on the basis of circumstances, but the underlying theme is in fact quite different. The theme is that peace and quiet equals death. The guilt for obtaining what should not have been obtained must be sabotaged. Peace is not deserved, gratification is not deserved, success is not deserved. In the service of relieving guilt it is essential to rescue, to repent, to pay a price. Sometimes the price is not only one's inability to experience pleasure and tranquility, but to even experience life itself.

Such an extreme example may lie in the life—and ultimately tragic death—of Primo Levi. He survived the concentration camps and became a great writer. He eventually committed suicide.

What is fear of success? Is there really such a phenomenon? Or has much been made of this, when in fact, it is simply a mirage? Maybe. Failure in business or the arts or any endeavor can be real— the result of a downturn in the stock market, of bad business advice, sometimes, simply bad luck. But when it happens again and again, something else entirely is at work. Often it is a gnawing feeling of guilt for having a better life than others, a sense that it is undeserved. To some, success is equated with vanquishing others, destroying others. Success becomes a dirty word, evidence that one is somehow getting away with something undeserved. It's difficult to own up to and accept accountability for success—*it must be a fluke, an accident. I can't believe my efforts paid off.* The underlying belief is that I don't deserve to succeed and if I do, I have to undo it, undermine it, mess it up. We talk of the fear of failure, but the fear of success is every bit as problematical.

Alan built a small specialty business that seemed to be doing well. The business required know-how about esoteric collectibles and he educated himself well. He developed a reputation as an expert in the field. However, just as the business was on verge of becoming what would, or could, have been a phenomenal success, he found himself sabotaging himself. He would go to the office and find busy work rather than do the important things that he knew needed doing. And this was not the first time. He had a history of starting projects, reaching a certain point of success and then losing interest.

In addition, things were not well in his marriage. As much as he loved his wife, he had avoided sexual relations with her for years. He did not understand why. His wife gave up complaining because Alan became evasive and defensive. They had both decided prior to marriage not to have children. His wife had a good career and devoted herself there, not wanting to press the issue of intimacy.

Alan entered therapy because he finally recognized that in his business he was at a crossroads and his personal life wasn't too great, either. After several months of therapy, Alan reported the following dream: "I'm watching a women's basketball game. The teams consisted of an Ivy League college team composed mostly of tall, white women. The other team was made up of short women from a distinctly inferior state college. The state college team won. I began to cry out of happiness that the state college team won." He reported that the winning team was considered the underdog in the league. The fact that the women on this team were all short led Alan to associate that they were the underdogs. He went on to say that he often rooted for the underdog and in real life became overwhelmed with tearful emotion when the underdog won. Why? Because he felt he was the underdog and thus felt an affinity for the underdog. He viewed his father as the winner, the top dog, in contrast to himself as the loser. He wanted to win, but couldn't. He needed someone else to be the winner so he could admire them and feel that, because they were the winner, they could take care of him. As the loser, Alan did not have to assume responsibility and he did not have to suffer the guilt of succeeding beyond his father.

Alan grew up, the oldest of three boys, cared for by a nanny. His mother was a career woman who was always busy. His father was successful, alcoholic, and exhibitionistic. He had to be top dog in the family. He was interested in talking about his successes and demonstrating how good he was. He was an expert sailor, a winning tennis player, very handy around the house. And he had no time or interest in his son. If Alan did something well, his father shrugged. *Not good enough*, he seemed to say. *I could have done much better.*

Alan was bright, but a gross underachiever in school. But no one cared. Alan didn't care either and didn't really try. Following his schooling, he became involved in some challenging activities that he was good at, but there was no future in these undertakings. They were more like challenging hobbies.

Alan felt that his father was the winner for many reasons, one of which was because he had his mother. Alan had strong desires for his mother whom he described as an exceptionally beautiful woman. His mother was the prize and, though he desired the prize, he knew it was forbidden. Success was a state to be desired but feared. It meant undertaking responsibilities he could never fulfill. Success and responsibility were for others and not for him. Yet, success involved responsibilities he yearned for but doubted he could ever fulfill, and he did not want to take the risk of trying. Instead, Alan became passive and detached.

The dynamics operating here are replicated in many different forms that are based upon a triangular situation between child and parent. There is the son who wants to supersede his father. There is the father who is threatened by his young son and must squash him and beat him at any competition. There is the mother who reminds the daughter that she, the mother, is the queen who plans to remain in the dominant position. The children of such relationships, the classical Oedipal triangle, often suffer guilt for their wishes and develop fears of succeeding. They sabotage themselves in a variety of ways. Here, again, the fantasy and the wish become equated with reality.

Athletes at the brink of success may falter and lose their standing. Young, talented prize-winning musicians develop serious blocks and cannot perform. Business executives who have worked hard to reach the top switch companies prior to a major promotion. The turning point in many of these cases is subjective, based upon a fantasy that going beyond a certain point is fraught with too much responsibility, too much exposure, and too much success. For such individuals, unless some insights intervene, sabotaging one's future success is the only way out of the dilemma.

In therapy, Alan was able to move ahead by developing insight into the underlying feelings that existed in relation to his family and the way they related to him. He was more attuned to his anger and longing for parents who could have supported him, but had neither the time nor the interest to do so. After a while, he was able to own up to the fact that his business was his and not his father's. He could see eventually that his success or failure was a function of his own behavior. He no longer had to feel guilty, nor did he have to perceive himself as the underdog. He finally deserved to win.

Alan's increasing successes in his business also reflected another dilemma. When he was able to close on deals in which his profit margin could have been greater than he thought it should be, he felt guilty. He even lowered the price on an item when he did not have to. He was very sensitive to being fair and he needed to assure himself that he was not taking advantage of anyone. In fact, when he learned of others in his business who were operating on a higher profit margin, he became troubled. Underlying all this, it emerged, was just the opposite motive. He really did not want to work, he just wanted a lot of money. But he was unable to accept his avaricious urges. In fact, Alan had trouble accepting his basic primitive urges to be competitive, to win, to get things easily. To his way of thinking, he was either a crook or a saint and there was no in-between. So he sided with being the saint by having to prove to himself that he fairly earned what he got.

Many people try to allay their fears of their more primitive urges for aggression, sex, hunger, and avarice not by owning them as part of being a human animal, but by denying them, by trying to be above such base impulses. They must be consummately civilized and refined. The problem is that we all have such urges and we all have to tame them in order to live in a civilized society. But if we persist in denying them, we are faced with conflicts that cause tension, guilt, and in some cases, failure.

Chapter 5

Repetitions on the Job

What do you want to be when you grow up? This question, asked repeatedly of children from the time they understand speech, is a clue to the premium we place on work. All children, whether prompted or not, ponder and explore, through play and imagination, what they might be when they finally grow up. They will change their minds a thousand times. They will copy their parents, or else reject their parents' choices. They may want to emulate a TV star, or pin their hopes on being the biggest, best basketball player ever—even while they are still only three feet tall. They have grandiose dreams: I will be an Olympic athlete first, because I am a good swimmer. Then, after I do that, I will be an attorney, and go to Washington and change all the bad laws. Or, I will be a rock star, and then a football player, but I won't be a doctor because they work too hard. I want to be a vet because I love animals and my dog is sick. Children view the world from their own tiny lenses, and often see and report back to us adults some amazing things and awesome insights. These insights are often insights into how their parents view their world and their jobs.

So how do children eventually find gratification in an endeavor that is likely to consume such a huge part of their future life? Will work be simply a means of earning a living, getting a paycheck, surviving financially? Or will it be a way of meeting challenges, of personal growth, or of realizing one's potentials? If one is lucky, and perhaps wise, one is able to choose work that fits one's personality, one's deep needs. It has been said that real maturity comes with finding fulfillment in love and work. But whatever one's job, whether there is choice or not, work usually entails interaction with others, even in this day when so many jobs are off-site. One still has to report to bosses, to colleagues, to customers, or clients. We know that regardless of how competent individuals are, how well they do their job, how much pleasure they get out of the work itself, problems can—almost always do—arise when any of us interact with others. Are we quick to settle for anything in order to please and find peace at any price? Are we competitive, intent on beating others out? Do we have preconceived ideas, unconscious expectations that those we work with are going to be cooperative or domineering or submissive? Are others out to get us?

Job success and job satisfaction are sometimes less a function of competence than of interpersonal relationships. Many of us know competent people have been replaced because they were irritants to others with whom they work. Many of us know of bright and talented people who never progress beyond a certain level because of their inability to get along with bosses or colleagues. Some of these people go from job to job blaming their difficulties on the people with whom they work. Yet, they go on to new jobs and find themselves with similar problems.

It's already clear by now that childhood experiences and family experiences color adult relationships. What is less well understood, perhaps, is that these early experiences also affect our relationships within the workplace. Thus the boss becomes the image of a parent; a colleague becomes a brother or sister. A stern father becomes an overbearing boss. A competitive sister becomes a bloodthirsty rival. These perceptions in the workplace are distorted by those early, unresolved problematic relationships. Until the perception is changed, individuals go on acting the same way, because they continue to perceive things the same way. A senior marketing executive continues to look for hidden agendas in everything his boss says—not because the boss is duplicitous, but because the executive's mother specialized in hidden agendas.

We bring ourselves to our jobs. We may be hard working and capable, but we bring our personalities, our histories, our early relationships with significant people to the job and, as the reader surely knows by now, we often tend to repeat those relationships in the workplace.

Just as we bring baggage with us into marriages, so we bring baggage from the past into the workplace. Howard began to talk about himself in a quiet, calm voice. He was thirty-five, happily married with two children. He had an MBA and was employed as a manager with a Fortune 500 company earning a six-figure salary plus a substantial annual bonus. This was his third job since he had completed graduate school about ten years earlier.

"I love my work and I'm good at it," he said.

Why had he left his two earlier jobs? "Nobody fired me. I left on my own." His competence was never questioned. However, he was told—though not in so many words that the "chemistry" was not right and that it might be better if he looked for another job. In heart-to-heart talks and in performance reviews, Howard was described as having an "abrasive personality." Howard's demeanor was anything but abrasive. But he was starting to get signals in his present job, as he had on previous jobs, that he was divisive, argumentative, difficult. He ran into these problems with coworkers, but most often with his boss. He didn't feel that he got the recognition he deserved or that his boss was supportive of his work.

Howard said, "Look, I'm a reasonable guy and I like to work things out rationally. But when my boss took my ideas and questioned my approach, I got livid." He acknowledged that he had run into similar problems previously and he decided that he had to do something about this. He said that he usually did not lose his temper, but that when roadblocks were put in his way and when his efforts were not recognized, he lost control and got into confrontations. While he was aware that his loss of control was a problem, he was certain that his rage reactions were provoked by others.

I asked Howard about his early life and he shrugged and smiled as if to say *all shrinks ask questions like this* but he might as well humor me. "You might say that I had an adventurous life," he replied.

Howard's father was an executive representing an American company with extensive overseas holdings. The unstable third world countries in which Howard grew up were in constant upheaval with rioting and looting. Though he was enrolled in an American school, he felt unprotected and at risk as did the rest of the family.

"My father was a rugged guy," Howard said. "That's why his company sent him to these hot spots." Howard's mother, however, did not take to the feverish third world atmosphere as well as her husband. She was angry with her husband and protective of her children, all of which created an atmosphere of tension in the family. Mother would say, "Why does he take us to these godforsaken places?" She was frightened, and, consequently, so were the children.

Howard's father expected his two sons to be as tough and macho as he was. "Dad was an awesome figure. He was really hard on me. I could never do anything to please him."

This was the start of Howard's psychotherapy. As we proceeded to unearth the real outlines of his early family life, certain patterns began to emerge and he was able to put them together. "In business you have to be a competitor and I learned about competition at my father's knee." Not only was his father competitive in business, but he competed with his son as well. His father was the one who exposed his wife and kids to a threatening environment. So he felt that he, as the father, had to fight the threats as well. The family was at war between two camps. Camp one consisted of mother and Howard and his younger sister who were on mother's side. Camp two consisted of father and older daughter and younger son who identified with father.

"I guess I was a pretty sensitive kid," Howard recalled. "I was even more sensitized by the feeling that I had to protect my mother and sister. After Dad, no boss could look too tough to take on." Howard's father bullied the entire family, blustering through all situations as the unquestioned authority. The rest of the family lived in a state of constant intimidation. They either cowered in fear and conformed in slavish surrender, or confronted him, as Howard did, the only outspoken one in the family. This placed him at odds with his father, but he would not give in to his father. Bullied and taunted by his father, Howard became enraged and vengeful. However, he learned to maintain a calm exterior unless provoked.

Because he could not express his anger freely, Howard projected his feelings onto others and especially those whom he saw as being unjust and bullying. He perceived the world, but more specifically those in power, as a threat. He could not let them get away with bullying him. He was compelled to confront them and take them on as adversaries. Since he had been traumatized by his father, he was hypervigilant to those who were in a position to undermine him.

Howard was very sensitive to slights. He needed to be recognized and when he felt ignored, or when he felt he was not given the credit he deserved, he became infuriated. His father treated him as if he was a nonperson and Howard could not tolerate reactions that took him and his accomplishments for granted. At times, he overreacted-even when there was little provocation. But he felt justified because in his mind, he was protecting what was right and just. He was protecting his mother. And he kept replaying this scenario again and again. He was protecting himself from a repetition of the treatment he received in the past.

But the self-defeating aspect lay in his overreactions and his extreme sensitivity. He was trying to gain mastery and to vanquish the unfair and hypocritical aggressor. To him it was a life-and-death struggle to prove to himself that he would not be unfairly dominated. He would not be undermined in his efforts to find a sense of autonomy, to be out from under the thumb of those who might take advantage of his weakness.

The underlying residue of anger and the sensitivity to being bullied were deeply entrenched. Howard needed to relate to someone whom he perceived to be in a position of authority, but who was not interested in bullying him. He needed someone who could understand him and his plight. And that's what he sought in his therapist. In the one-on-one relationship with someone able to listen to him, free of judgment, he was able to grasp the repetitive and self-destructive nature of his behavior toward those in the workplace. He could understand and work through his hostility toward his father. As his relationship with his father became less important to him, he was able to deal more equitably with challenges—though he still could not brook those who were aggressively demeaning to him.

Under certain circumstances, it is necessary to get some distance from the provoking agent. Howard chose to find a position where he could work off-site, at a distance from his boss to relieve the constant aggravation and provocation of one-to-one contact. Gradually, he was able to relate to authority figures on a more equal basis. He was able to accept the fact that he could have gone further in his profession if he did not have to carry the burdens of his angers and resentments. But he was thankful that he reached a point of being able to deal more easily with those in authority.

Arthur was an accountant, tops in his field, a field that required attention to every detail. Arthur was a precise and meticulous person and such personality traits were a major asset on his job. He passed the several examinations required by his profession to be expert. He worked hard and the results of his work were excellent. However, he constantly came into conflict with others who were lax, who made mistakes, who did not work as long, as hard, or as carefully as he did. With intense righteous indignation, he was critical of coworkers and bosses who were not as competent and industrious as he was, yet held more senior positions. Small things made him furious. He lost his temper at imagined slights, which placed him in conflict again and again. At the same time, he was very sensitive to any hint that he was not appreciated for all that he did. He felt he was a victim, a martyr, the one who sacrificed for everyone. He chronically felt overwhelmed and overburdened as though it was up to him and only him to get the job done right. In his mind, he was indispensable. However, when there were slow periods, he felt wasted, feeling that he was working below his capacities. Once, he changed jobs because he was furious that his company did not give him the bonus he felt he deserved. Then he did it again. And again. However, with every new job, there came a time when there was a repetition of the same problem, the same fury.

Something was wrong. And Arthur was bright enough to sense it. And so he came for therapy. Almost immediately, after detailing the current problem, he began to talk about his father.

"My father gave everything to my sister," he said. "He overlooked her failures, but not so for me. He gave me nothing but criticism and nastiness." He described his father as intelligent and socially active, but stingy and spiteful. "I tried like the devil to please him and never could. My sister screwed up all over the place and he'd just bail her out of one goof after the next." His parents divorced when he was in middle school and according to Arthur that was a blessing. They had never gotten along, fought constantly, and, at least in Arthur's eyes, they took it all out on him.

"Splitting" is a term that describes a tendency to see people as good or bad, right or wrong, black or white, and this is what Arthur did. His mother was kind and considerate—or cold, suspicious, and dissatisfied. She was always looking for evidence that she was being cheated. His father was intelligent, but mean and vengeful. His relationship with his wife was also one of splitting. She was quiet, kind, and caring—or incompetent and careless.

This splitting carried over to the job where one boss after the other was good and then bad, as were coworkers. Arthur felt constantly torn. There was always agitation and unrest. It was as though he could not feel alive and real unless there was constant stimulation, usually based upon irritation. Arthur was looking for the magic that would make everything right. The prospect of a new job meant that all his troubles would be over, that he would be appreciated, and that he would be respected. But it didn't take long before troubles began with new bosses and coworkers. He began to scrutinize and criticize everyone. He was vigilant, always expecting someone to do him wrong.

On some occasions, he came to his session a few minutes late. "I know I'm late, but can you make up the time?" he would ask.

"The session is forty-five minutes," I replied.

He insisted that he was entitled to the full session. I explained that running overtime with him would mean keeping others waiting and would disrupt my schedule. He did not care. He wanted his time despite the fact that it was he who was late. He was incapable of seeing the impact of his behavior on others. He had little concern or empathy for others.

Arthur earned a very good living, but he lived frugally, constantly worried that he wouldn't be able to make ends meet. "They try to rip me off everywhere. I always check my bills because they make mistakes and when I catch a mistake, I let them know about it."

Deprivation was the key word. Arthur never got enough and most people did not treat him fairly. His bonus was higher than his coworkers, but according to him, it should have been higher.

I earned it. I worked harder than they did by far and my bonus was only a fraction of what it should have been. Others get away with everything. Coworkers and bosses are incompetent. They take liberties while I check and recheck everything.

This attitude was evident to those around him. "No one wants to join me for lunch," he said once. "I'm never asked to go out with the others after work, but who would want to spend more time with those jerks anyway?"

It was hard for Arthur to grasp the idea that his attitudes permeated the way he related. Although he claimed never to have said such things out loud, he could not understand the concept of nonverbal communication. He was utterly unable to put himself in anyone else's position. Situations were as he saw them and anyone who viewed things differently was wrong.

Arthur was angry. His mother had been angry. His father had been angry. It took a lot of work for Arthur to see all this and to let his feelings of hurt and disappointment become real to him, more real than words alone. There are other dynamics operating in the case of Arthur. Arthur experienced his growing up—his deprivations, the unfavorable treatment he received compared with his sister—as a slap in the face to him. The punitive and harsh treatment became a template for the way he dealt with himself and the rest of the world. There was no room for Arthur to express the anger that was building up within him at his parents. He was certain that such expression would not be tolerated. As a result, he developed a punishing sense of conscience. His world was divided into right or wrong, good or bad and he had to be good, he had to be right. He had to be right or the consequences would have been punishment and disapproval. And that, he could not tolerate.

Finally, largely through the work of therapy, Arthur became aware of his egocentric view of the world. He began to see connections between the way he felt he had been treated by his parents and the way his parents interacted with each other and with the world around them. Gradually, he appreciated that while he viewed the world as black or white, right or wrong, most of life, and particularly relationships, was not that way. He began to see that not all situations could be reduced to black or white.

A true moment of change occurred when Arthur was raging to me about his boss. I interjected with the following remark: "My interpretations may not always be right on the mark, but your reaction to your boss could be viewed differently than the way you see it."

"What do you mean, you don't know if you're right or not?" he cried.

I didn't reply.

"Don't you know what you're doing?" he asked. "How can I trust you if your remarks aren't correct?"

"I try to understand you, but that's not always easy," I said.

Arthur was stunned. He had never allowed for such a possibility. He had never considered looking at relationships in any way other than his way. He was severely self-centered and I remarked to him, "You defend yourself against possible criticism by shutting off alternative explanations. You must believe that you are right, because you view things as right or wrong without considering other possibilities. To you, you must be right, because if you're not right, then you're wrong and that would leave you open to negative judgment. But by seeing things your way, you exclude the possibility of alternative explanations. None of us, not you, not me, is right all of the time."

I also added that this need for me to always be right really exposed his intense dependency, his need for someone infallible to depend on. It was slow. Oh, it was slow. But eventually, Arthur began to become more open-minded. With his wife particularly, his critical rages diminished as he began to listen to her explanations as to why she had to buy something or to do something. The hard edge began to soften. His anger at his parents continued, but he was more open and forgiving with people at work. His sense of emptiness and of being cheated receded, and he realized that while some people might be out to take advantage of him, he could not generalize and assume that everyone was.

Arthur began to realize the degree to which he identified with each of his parents. He saw how their conflicts between each other became his inner conflicts that were projected onto the environment. His tendency to take sides, to see one person as OK and another one at fault, represented his expectation, indeed his need, to perpetuate the conflicts that he grew up with. Unconsciously, his perceptions and his actions were based upon a self-fulfilling prophecy—that is, that the world at large was a reproduction of his primary family. He expected to find warring factions and he found them. He expected to be taken advantage of and he found that he was. He expected to be cheated and he found reasons to convince himself that he was being cheated.

He now viewed his parents as unhappy people and he was able to be more distant and more objective about them. Instead of taking them seriously, he was able to take a step aside and not get into arguments with them. As he became more of an outside observer, he was in a better position to evaluate the very characteristics that he saw and disliked in himself. His contacts with his parents became less frequent, and as he did so, there was a process of sadness and regrets. There was sadness at how hurt he had been by them and he had regrets at all the pain he endured because of his identification with them. He had regrets at his impatience and rages at others that he now realized were not warranted. The interesting thing about his distancing from his parents was that this just seemed to happen. He did not force himself to be less involved with them. Instead, contact with them became less fulfilling and less desirable. He was able to focus more on his immediate family and his work. He took things more in stride and no longer looked for a sudden cure-all to make everything better. Arthur was maturing by becoming less self-absorbed. Sadly, he could not look to his parents for approval or solace because that was only forthcoming as long as he complained about the injustices and insults heaped upon him by others—attitudes that coincided with the attitudes fostered by his parents. This price was too high for the little support he received by being the victim. He no longer saw this position as desirable for him. He suffered much in the process, but the suffering was infinitely preferable to the sad and defensive way he had been leading his life. He became, finally, the person he wanted to be, the adult who could enjoy life and relationships. Even if they weren't perfect.

People like Arthur and Fred suffer intense feelings of guilt. They punish themselves, preventing themselves from being nice to themselves, preventing themselves from enjoying life. They are tense and fearful, feeling as though they are living under a microscope where their every thought, action, or feeling is scrutinized. They are fearful of their basic human condition—that is, their feelings, dreams, fantasies—because they have been exposed to such intense rages and punishments themselves. They are sure that if they relax, they will think, do, or feel bad things. Then they will suffer the wrath of greater powers. In order to protect themselves from themselves, in order to protect others from their intense anger, they must be perfect. Because of this state of torment and tension they get themselves into situations in which the feared punishment sometimes becomes a reality. The tension causes strains on the body in the form of physical complaints. The tension causes problems with others. Passive-aggressive behavior may also be manifested so that others are offended by things that are said or done. The individual is unable to understand why others avoid him—since he fails to grasp the hostile nature of his behavior. He feels he is innocent. Thus the fear of punishment causes the very thing that is feared.

There is another reaction, however, to this fear of severe punishment that is quite the opposite. That reaction can be one of defiance, rebelliousness, and risky behavior. Such individuals do not care how others feel. They act out their feelings without regard to the consequences. The result is that these people get into trouble again and again, but they feel justified. It may be recalled that Fred tried to please his demanding and punitive parents until he finally gave up on them. He began acting in defiant and possibly dangerous ways, on the brink of doing things that could have caused havoc in his life. Fortunately, he was able to see this behavior for what it was. He, like Arthur, was able to change. They were both able to deal with their mistreatment—as well as their resulting anger.

Samantha was a totally different story. To begin, there are two things to note about Samantha. First, she was a stunningly beautiful woman. And second, she had absolutely no idea that she was. Never have I met someone in whom there was such a discrepancy between her outer and inner perception of herself.

She came to me with a very practical concern. "I'm having a little trouble prioritizing my time, my tasks, and my objectives," she told me the minute she settled down in my office. "Maybe you could help me learn a formula for making a 'to-do' list every day to make sure I get everything done. My house is a mess. I have papers all over the place. I can't stand it and neither can my husband."

It seemed to me that this was an oddly limited request. It did not seem that such a relatively simple skill would elude a woman of Sam's obvious intelligence and accomplishment. At forty, she was doing well in her marketing job with a Fortune 500 corporation. She had graduated from a good college and good business school, and then managed to get a job, against intense competition, with a large, high-powered firm. Some of her work there had been brilliant. But she had noticed that despite her good reviews and decent bonuses, others were being promoted over her to high-level positions. Though it was never made explicit, she got the message that her work was not as well organized as it could have been.

When I began to probe deeper into her background and childhood, Sam became impatient with me. She wanted to stay focused on the problem at hand, and that was, to her, time management.

Now, some patients are like that. For one thing, managed care has encouraged people to break off their mental health problems into tiny-sized chunks, to have a specific focus that can be corrected in short order. For others, the pressure comes from within. They want to define and control the problem in order to avoid probing any deeper. And many therapists of different persuasions go along with this. They prefer to deal with immediate behavior issues. In fact, Sam had previously gone to someone who gave her suggestions on time management and offered hints on how she could get the mess at home cleared up by doing things one at a time in step-by-step fashion. Still, it wasn't long before Sam was back where she started. And so she started again, by coming to me.

"You're trying to put a Band-Aid on a larger problem," I said after she told me a little about her background. I touched on things she told me about her history and I tried to offer some connections. Though she didn't want to hear it, she had to admit that she had never seen the relationship between her present symptoms and her past. I mentioned that the kind of therapy that I do calls for recognizing how the present is related to her past. I said we had to get a dynamic grasp on the underpinnings of her behavior. Only by doing this, I said, could she really get a solid handle on the problem.

She decided to think about it. I didn't hear from her for a few weeks, but I had a strong feeling that she would be back, and, in fact, she did return.

"I'm not happy about this process," she said. "But I have to do something and the other route didn't work. So here I am." She said it with an air of anxious resignation.

What had not been so obvious earlier was Sam's high level of anxiety. She spoke under pressure and let loose a barrage of concerns as to where this might lead, her concerns about being detoured from her goals of dealing better with time and organization.

"You're afraid of finding some things about yourself that you might not want to know?" I asked.

She agreed but had to admit that she didn't know what that could be. I told her that some issues underlay her anxious behavior resulting in her time management and organizational problems. I explained that I was not a mind reader and did not know what we would discover, but that we would go down this road of exploration together. The tools for accomplishing this process of discovery required that she try to say whatever came to mind and to bring in her dreams. Sam was quick to remark that this didn't make any sense to her at all, but she would try, at which point she recalled a dream she had had a couple of nights before.

Prior to discussing Sam's dream, something must be said about dreams and their place in psychodynamic psychotherapy. Dreams play a crucial part in aiding the resolution of repetitious, self-sabotaging personality patterns as they do in psychotherapy generally. Dream interpretation has been the butt of many jokes and cartoons, but to paraphrase Freud, *people deny my theories by day, but they dream them at night.*

Dreams are the "royal road to the unconscious,"[1] a potent way of aiding in the process of making what is unconscious conscious. The significance of dreams has more recently been substantiated by findings in neuroscience.

The process of ownership of one's inner life and behavior through dreams is one of unraveling a riddle, solving a puzzle. Dreams are not only messages from the unconscious, but they also serve to advance therapy. Repetitive dreams with the same themes indicate that the same problem is still present and is still yearning to be attended to and to be worked through. The art of dream interpretation requires detective work. Dreams and the dreamer's associations to the dreams represent clues, hints as to what is going on in the mind of the dreamer.

Dreams are stimulated and triggered by events of the day, but every dream is a part of the present, which resonates with the past. Of all the stimuli that impinge upon us in the course of the day, we choose some event, often apparently insignificant, as the stuff of which to dream. It could be meeting someone, hearing something, seeing something on television, which appears in the dream. The associations remind us of someone significant in our lives, an event that was important in our lives. Dreams camouflage, condense, substitute one person for another, one event for another. The dreamer's associations are all-important. That's why it's risky to try to interpret a dream from the surface content. Instead, the elements in the dream are to be viewed as springboards for associations that stimulate memories, fantasies, and wishes hidden from us. We dream of people and events from decades ago whom we have not thought of for years, but who have significance, if only to arouse other thoughts and feelings and memories. Dreams are a way of telling us what's on our minds. They bring to the fore material that bridges the present with the past. And once we associate to the dream, we are faced with the fact that we are the dreamer. Though we may try to disavow certain fantasies, when we dream them, we have no choice but to recognize that they are part of us. Often we dismiss things because *it's only a dream* but we have to own up to the fact that our dreams are created by us, that every person or event in the dream is part of who we are. We cannot deny that these thoughts are coming from within us. I'm not talking about the surface content of the dream, but rather the associations, memories, thoughts, and feelings that come from analyzing and seeing the dream in all of its ramifications. Some dreams are scary and some are soothing, some are funny and some expose deep-seated fears and anxieties.

Whatever emerges indicates where we are within our thoughts, within our relationships. The more dreams are opened up to the fresh air of analysis, the more helpful they are, as if we are bringing secrets out that surprise even us, the dreamer. And we know that the more those secrets are kept hidden, the less likely it is that change will occur. In contrast, the more those secrets are brought out, as embarrassing or shameful as they seem, the more the way to change is paved by bringing them to the surface, the better we will know who we are. How often has a new patient balked at exposing fantasies and dreams, at entering psychoanalysis because *I'm afraid of what I might discover.* And the reply may be: Are you better off knowing or not knowing? Are you saying that you are fearful of discovering who you are? Do you want to continue hiding from yourself in fear? Many would reply that they are better off leaving things the way they are. However, there are others who want to discover as much as they can about themselves.

In Sam's dream:

"I was sitting in a doctor's office. I was nude and had a long velour robe on. I was on an examining table and you were there. I couldn't get down from the table without the robe opening, but I managed it. You were fully dressed with a tweed jacket. You came over and put your arm around me. I was frightened and said, 'I don't like men.'" "I woke up and felt anxious upon awakening."

Since this was Sam's first dream, I explained to her how we work with dreams. I told her that I will mention a word or phrase from the dream and that she should use this word or phrase as a springboard to say whatever came to mind out of context of the dream. I asked her about the phrase, "I don't like men." Reluctantly, she spoke about her husband and her father.

The first dream reported in therapy frequently provides important clues for the future and that was true for Sam. Her high achievements were in the service of proving her self-worth and her ability to overcome adversity.

It would take months before Sam came to see that her "time management" problems were related to her concerns about maintaining obsessive control over everything and leaving nothing to chance. She had to maintain constant vigilance lest her wishes, fears, and impulses crept through. In her quest to assert control, she defeated herself. Being messy also meant to her that she was not giving in to pressure, that she would do what she wanted, when she wanted, and the way she wanted. She would not just give others what they wanted, but would stand up for herself even at the price of defeating herself. She would no longer just submit to "get it over with."

As we worked together, I learned much about Sam's background, and with it, the hurts that had led to her current problems which, in fact, were elaborations on her first dream in therapy and represented continuing associations to the phrase, "I don't like men." Before her birth, her parents had wanted a boy and chose the name Sam. When the baby was born a girl, the name shift to Samantha was easy, but shifting identity was not. Sam always felt she was a disappointment to her parents, perhaps the reason that she never really felt beautiful. The attention of men served to increase her resentments—as she felt she was being viewed as a sexual object. Yet she used sex to win love and power. This was fostered by her mother's extramarital affairs that Samantha knew about from the time she was very small. It was furthered by her mother's abandoning her when Sam was just fourteen. She left Sam with the father, while she took Samantha's younger siblings with her to live with another man. Her father had little time or interest in parenting her. He was a bitter, lonely man who was more interested in his own situation than he was in tending to his daughter. And so, from the age of fourteen on, Samantha raised herself.

She wanted to do well in school and she did, because she was very bright. But she was lonely and hungry for attention. Her attractiveness made her the center of attention from boys and her neediness made her an easy mark for their sexual advances. Being abandoned by her mother as she entered adolescence and left to live alone with her father only exacerbated her tendency to sexualize relationships. There were no sexual traumas with her father, but the very act of living alone in an apartment with her father was a fertile ground for oedipal fantasies and wishes that she could not understand. This, together with her mother's sexual behavior, made it difficult for Sam to deal with issues of growing up to be a woman.

Her marriage took place shortly after her college graduation. Her husband was fifteen years older than she was and appeared to be able to provide her with the stability, strength, and interest that she longed for. He had been married before and had children of that previous marriage. He was successful, but Sam was struck by his devotion to his children and assumed that he would be as devoted to her. Indeed, he was devoted to his children but he was also very ambitious and very busy and had little time for her. Though she worked, she was lonely again living with a man who, like her father, had little time to devote to her. She became obsessed with sexual thoughts about other men which she tried to put to rest by getting a good but very demanding job and working very hard. But she had trouble managing her time.

Prior to her marriage, she had felt lonely and her sexual behavior bordered on the promiscuous. Now, she feared she would stray from the marriage. The trauma of abandonment had never left Sam and played itself out in her desire to frequently test the limits of other people's affection for her. Would they abandon her too? She recalled feeling this way in college and graduate school, but at that time, she sought release through her sexual escapades and was then able to return to her studies. Now, she sensed that she was at risk of destroying her career as well as her marriage as her mother had destroyed her own.

Sam communicated very contradictory messages in the course of her treatment. She wanted to allow herself to be dependent, but as soon as this happened, she would pull away. When she became open and expressive of her feelings and her needs, she would back off and attempt to assure herself that she did not need an involved relationship with the therapist. She yearned to be passive and to allow herself to submit to her thoughts and feelings, only to announce that she was feeling better and able to go it alone. She took what I call, "flights into health"—*I'm fine, don't need you, I feel better*—as a means of not revealing her underlying feelings and desires. When she was asked to use the couch, she did so reluctantly and expressed strong feelings about being placed in a dependent position, fearful that she would be exposed and vulnerable.

She announced on more than one occasion, "I don't want to need you. I *don't* need you!"

But the next session would have her asking, "I want you to hold me. I want you to love me."

But could we discuss these ambivalent messages? Not easily. Efforts to talk about this were met with her rage and frustration, with feelings of abandonment and isolation at not getting what she wanted. She was a frightened child who needed physical contact, but that was sexualized and frightening. She was proving that her needs could not be met. Talk was cheap and it was not what she yearned for. She was unable to accept her dependent needs because dependency immediately became sexualized and could only be warded off by assuring herself of her independence and personal competency.

She could not trust others because she could not trust herself. She felt that when she turned for help, she would get sex. Yet she wanted sex—a wish to give in to her dependency needs, but also a wish to get it out of the way. Sex was inevitable. So she might as well get it over with. This led in turn to seductive behavior, followed by fantasies of working with a female therapist so she would not have to deal with this. However, she dismissed this because women were not to be trusted. They would abandon her as her mother had.

It was only by repeatedly dealing with these feelings and her seductive efforts, her doing and undoing, the side-by-side juxtaposition of opposing urges that she eventually made progress. It began when she tried to seduce me. She would not just lie on the couch and free associate. She wore revealing clothing; she would squirm around on the couch while talking of sexual encounters with her husband, what she would do to him and what he would do to her. All of this was an attempt to arouse the therapist. If she succeeded in this, it would be a repetition of her belief that she could not be appreciated without sexual involvement. It would have confirmed the feeling that her mother was "messy" and that she was "messy" too. She spoke of feelings that sexual encounters were contaminating and dirty.

It is always difficult, but imperative, for a therapist to deal with these issues, and neutrality and objectivity were necessary. This neutral stance gradually brought about a realization in Samantha that men could be understanding, could be attentive and warm and not become sexually involved. "You seem to be rather restless today," I commented once. "Perhaps the clothes you are wearing aren't comfortable."

She became furious. Frustrated. It was the only time her sexual machinations were explicitly exposed as a maneuver on her part to prove that no man could be trusted, and, more importantly, that she could not be trusted to have a caring relationship that would not culminate in sex. She could be appreciated for herself without ambivalence and without demands being made of her.

The significance of our work together resulted in Samantha's shifting of her interest away from her job in the marketing field. She really hadn't liked it anyway. She now wanted to work with people, especially with adolescent girls, for she certainly knew first hand what kinds of problems those girls might have. She wanted to get a degree in social work, but that would mean a return to school. No problem.

When she returned to me after several years, just kind of a "checkup" as she called it, she told me she had completed graduate schoolwork and was much happier in her new career.

She also had no problems with time management.

Chapter 6

Repetitions in the Addictions

DRUG ADDICTIONS

Any discussion of self-sabotaging cycles must include substance abuse, not only because of its frequency, but also because of the damage that is done to the individual abuser, as well as to the individual's family and friends. It can safely be said that all substance abuse affects not only the whole individual, but the entire family.

Substance abuse is not a unitary concept because in some instances it is physiologically based, while in others it is psychologically based. But whatever the causal factors may be, there are psychophysiological factors operating. Perhaps in no other area do we see the breakdown of the mind-body connection so clearly. Freud[1] predicted that some day a biological basis for neuroses would be discovered. This seems to be coming true, as almost every day we are making advances in neuroscience. Recently, for example, it has been found that some forms of dopamine given to patients with Parkinson's, to control the tremors of the disease, cause them to develop compulsive behavior. In some cases the compulsiveness is related to eating,[2,3] in others, drug abuse. More recently, it has been found that the use of some forms of dopamine causes compulsive gambling—even when this compulsion did not exist prior to the use of dopamine. The portions of the brain implicated in the processing of dopamine have been mapped and identified. The obvious question is whether there are biochemical aspects to other forms of compulsive behavior and does this apply to some forms of the repetition compulsion?

It seems likely that some types of compulsive behavior are more heavily weighted in the direction of psychological factors, while others are more heavily weighted in the direction of physiological and biochemical factors affecting brain functioning and the behavior that follows.

Up till now, we have viewed symptoms as a manifestation of deeper problems. We have examined the history, the background, the underlying motives and feelings in order to resolve the repetitions. However, in the case of the addictions we must view this differently. Here, the symptoms are so overwhelming and debilitating that the symptoms themselves must be addressed first. Therapy cannot be successfully conducted as long as these symptoms are operating. Because of this, when patients are referred for substance abuse issues, I tell them:

1. I cannot work with you as long as you are abusing drugs or alcohol,
2. It is crucial that you become engaged in a 12-step program, and
3. After you have stopped the abuse and have been actively engaged in a 12-step program, please call me and I will be glad to work with you.

I do this because one-on-one therapy cannot succeed when the patient is abusing drugs and the most effective treatment is a combination of engagement in the 12 steps plus psychotherapy after the drug abuse is terminated.

The reason for this lies in the configuration of psycho-physiological interactions. When discussing substance abuse, we must face the fact that, for the most part, the addictions are an exception to other forms of psychotherapeutic intervention, especially those addictions where the contribution of physical factors is greater than the emotional factors. For example, in most instances of alcoholism there is a family history of alcohol abuse. In some instances, one has the impression that the alcoholic has an almost "allergic" reaction to alcohol. Alcohol is the equivalent to walking through a patch of poison ivy. For most people, poison ivy is to be avoided because the results are clear.

One is going to get a terrible itchy rash that is going to cause serious discomfort. The answer is to avoid poison ivy. This is a physiological reaction. If one persists repeatedly in walking through poison ivy, there have to be self-punishing characteristics.

So it is with people who know that sensitivity to alcohol is familial, that there is a hereditary tilt in the direction of alcohol addiction with dire consequences. They are aware first hand of the effects of alcoholism. They know that, as children of an alcoholic, they are clearly at risk of becoming alcoholic. But they drink to excess, repeating the very destructive life that their parent lived. There are so many examples of families disrupted and of divorce and trauma to children because of alcoholism that examples are unnecessary.

Many alcoholics, of course, deny that their drinking is a problem. They point out that they show up for work every day, they come home every night—no problem. They do not focus on what happens when they come home. They drink and they become abusive. Or, they drink and one night they are abusive, and the next, they are mellow. Their behavior is so unpredictable that no one can count on them; no one knows what to expect. Some people face up to their alcoholism following a DWI, others wake up when they fall drunk in the gutter. Some require the intervention of family members uniting and confronting them with their alcoholism and with the damage that their drinking is doing to themselves and to those who care about them. Some join AA, while others persistently refuse. Others, in desperation, go to rehabilitation centers and emerge sober with the continuing help of AA. Others emerge sober only to begin drinking all over again.

There are instances where there is no family history and, by implication, no hereditary background. Here, the contribution of emotional factors to the alcoholism is greater than that of physical factors. Some of these individuals are able to stop their drinking "cold turkey." They are able to force themselves to stop drinking on their own, though it is difficult and long-term results are questionable.

Similarly, marijuana is generally not considered to be physiologically based though there are physical consequences. Persistent and repetitive use of marijuana affects one's motivation and drive, affects one's family life, and often one's job performance.

Al was a thirty-year-old married man who began using pot in high school. Though he was intelligent, he was unable to complete his school assignments and did not graduate. He did eventually get an equivalency diploma and entered a training program in electronics. He learned quickly and was good at this "hands-on" job, though he had difficulty staying with one company for any length of time. He was not happy with his work, feeling bored and restless. He smoked pot every night and every weekend. He said it was his only form of escape from his humdrum existence. He had friends, all of whom were pot smokers as well. He could have gone on this way but one of his supervisors became aware of what Al was doing. He took Al aside. He explained to him that he had a future with this company with opportunities for advancement, but not at the rate he was going. He related Al's work limitations to his pot smoking. At about the same time, Al became involved with a girl he cared for. She also became aware of his heavy use of marijuana and told him that she could not continue the relationship under these circumstances. The confluence of these two experiences seemed to hit home. He was upsetting his girlfriend and he was jeopardizing his occupational future more than he realized. Al was able to stop using marijuana. Of course, there are psychodynamics behind Al's abuse of marijuana, but he was not interested in delving into his background or his reasons for needing to escape. He wanted to move ahead in his occupation and he wanted to keep his girlfriend and that was enough to end his misuse of pot.

In contrast to marijuana, there are drugs that mimic and sometimes precipitate psychotic episodes, sometimes even resulting in suicide. The hallucinogens, LSD, peyote, and mescaline not only cause hallucinations, but also depression, paranoid ideation, perceptual distortions, and other defects in cognition. And there are serious "flashbacks," recurring experiences of these drug-induced symptoms that last long after the use of the hallucinogen has stopped.

We live in a drug culture. With the proliferation of drugs on the market, drugs that are used for medicinal purposes, there is an enormous opportunity for misuse of drugs. Pharmaceuticals prescribed for therapeutic purposes, for pain relief, for tranquilization, for relief from anxiety and depression may become addictive and may be misused. They find their way into the hands of children or are bought on the street, causing disorders in a variety of ways.

James was in a motorcycle accident. He broke some bones and was in pain. Percoset was prescribed to provide relief. He became addicted and continued to get prescriptions filled wherever he could. He missed work on his construction job. He was fired. He was driven to illegal means to get money in order to feed his habit. He swore that he would not use it any more when his wife demanded that he go to therapy. He did not use the drug for a week. He came to therapy swearing that he was no longer using it—but indeed, he was. He stopped therapy. I can only assume that things for James continued downhill.

This scenario can be repeated in the use of cocaine, crack cocaine, heroin, etc. We all know of the criminal involvement of people desperate to get money to buy drugs and of the terrible consequences of not being able to pay dealers for drugs that were obtained.

GAMBLING AND SEX ADDICTION

Is it too obvious to say that gambling ruins lives? Some people gamble as an escape from the pressures of daily life, while others gamble to prove to themselves that they can beat the odds. Whatever the motive, the results can be devastating. The gambling addict cannot stop, simply because he is an addict. He goes back for more, believing that this time, next time, he will win over the house. *I've got a new formula that's fail proof.* So goes the refrain. So goes hope.

The need here is to prove that one can win, all the while knowing that one is going to lose. There are neurochemical changes that occur when one gambles addictively. The gambler certainly gets a "high" not unlike that of the drug or alcohol addict. There is the challenge, the excitement, the sense of living on the edge.

A similar scenario is at work with the sex addict. He looks for excitement, even the illusion of love. Feeling like an impotent failure, the sex addict spends time and money seeking excitement and love[4] at strip bars or at places on or off the Web sites that offer pornography. Such an addict lives with the illusion that the women are really his, that they are taken with him. He knows better, but is helpless to stop. Wives and families discover this and home life is left in shambles.

Myron was an art professor at a prestigious college. Married with two children, he had all the accoutrements of success. He came from a background where his father was passive and compliant. His mother basically had no use for her husband and doted on Myron, her only son. Her doting bordered on the seductive. She sacrificed for, and praised, her talented son. Myron was able to get scholarships based upon his art. He went to fine art schools and eventually got a job at a good college. Over the years he was promoted to the head of the art department. He had married a woman who was successful in real estate and earned enough money so that their combined income allowed them to live a very comfortable life. But Myron harbored strong sexual urges that he could not satisfy in the marriage, though his wife never rejected his sexual advances. He needed more and more variety. His judgment was intact enough so that he did not risk seeking sexual contact with his students, though he was tempted and fantasized. He also did not risk seeking sex from the attractive models in his drawing classes. But he did frequent "strip joints," engaging the women there in personal friendships beyond the sexual contact. He believed they were taken by him. He spent hours watching pornography. Finally, his use of the family computer to feed his compulsion for pornography was his undoing. His wife and children discovered this and they were very upset about it. At their urging, he came for therapy. The dynamics behind his sexual preoccupations were uncovered, but he was still unable to curb his intense need to seek out sexually stimulating experiences. I urged him to attend a 12-step program for sexual addition because it became clear that understanding the dynamics of his background was not enough.

Many people suffer from inner hungers that get translated into addictions. And it is not just alcohol or drugs—it can also be food. Overweight people get caught up in cycles of yo-yo dieting. They gain and lose repeatedly. Obesity is related to one's body image and one's self-image. However, it is more than just image. Part of the conflict resides in the need to be in control. And this, this need to be in control, contradicts the wish to be free, to be able to beat the arrow on the scale.

Intellectually, most overweight people know that eating certain foods will lead to a gain in weight, but they play a game of roulette.

The conflict centers on an internal battle: *I want to eat it, but I know that it's not in my best interests to eat it. What? No way. No one is going to tell me what I can and cannot eat. I'll eat what I want.* There is a quality of defiance here. That is because dieting is not owned as part of the self. Rather, it is experienced as an outside force or person badgering one not to eat foods that will cause weight gain. It is experienced as if some authority figure is telling the individual what to do. Most people don't like to be told what to do. They are not happy with their obesity. They know it is destructive for their health and their image of themselves. But until they are able to avow the overweight as theirs, they will persist in fighting the diet. They may spend a good deal of money and time attempting to lose weight, only to gain it back again. In many respects, there is an adolescent conflict operating, one in which the drive for independence and autonomy is intense (*I'll do it my way on my own*) followed by a flight into conformity and dependence (*I gained all the weight back, so tell me what to do*) followed by rebellion (*Don't tell me what to do*). Add to this an addiction for sugar and the stage is set for the vicious cycle of weight gain and loss, weight gain and loss, ad infinitum.

In addition to the disavowal of accountability for overweight are the many rationalizations that people create. *It's my metabolism, my bone structure, the food that is in the house, I have to eat out a lot as part of my job, I have too much stress, I really don't eat very much, it's because of my pregnancies.* All of these represent ways of avoiding coming to grips with the problem emotionally. Overweight people are needy and are seeking ways to gratify their neediness, only to defeat themselves by being shunned socially and by feeling badly about themselves. The causes of their neediness will not be satisfied by eating more. The feeling of being full, or strong, or protected by a layer of fat is illusory.

Eric was a fifty-year-old markedly obese, depressed, divorced man who felt helpless and hopeless about himself. The last time he felt good about himself, he said, was when he was an inpatient for one month in a famous clinic. He lost thirty pounds. After he left the clinic, he gained the weight back, lost his job, and felt helpless. His depressed feelings had always been with him, but got worse following his divorce from his wife of fifteen years whom he said he married because, "I settled for her. I never thought anyone else would want me."

His parents had divorced when he was thirteen and he felt that he never really resolved his feelings about his parents' divorce. He said that he became more pessimistic since that time, always expecting that the worst would happen to him. As an adolescent, he lost trust and faith in his parents setting the stage for alternating attempts to become independent of his parents (who didn't know what they wanted) to being a child who needed guidance and direction.

Eric said, "Things get in the way of my doing what I want. I never feel that I'm being the person I want to be." Efforts to probe more deeply into this were met with avoidance. He wanted to talk about his job, his children, his depressed feelings. When I pointed this out to him, he became clearly uncomfortable. In the course of twelve therapy sessions, he lost a considerable amount of weight (though, according to him, that is not why he entered therapy.) However, he regained the weight. Again, he told me, "I let others define who I am or who I should be."

Interesting, because he began to perceive therapy as telling him who he should be—though no word of advice was ever given. This was his wish that someone would tell him what to do to satisfy his dependency needs. Eric was constantly doing and undoing. He admitted wanting immediate short-term gratification. I told him that I did not have that magic bullet that he was looking for. He had never resolved his basic ambivalence and confusion around being the unhappy dependent child vs. the independent adult.

After some time, he arranged to undergo bariatric surgery. However, this was at the same time that he had begun to lose weight again. He had no patience with working through his problems.

This case clearly points up some of the dynamics that have been discussed. He was extremely needy, but did not take responsibility for his situation or his actions. And he did not have the patience and tolerance for frustration necessary to exert the long-term effort that would be needed to work through his problems. He reenacted in the therapeutic relationship his basic conflict between wanting someone to tell him what to do and wanting to do things his own way. He did take steps to obtain help by going to the clinic and entering psychotherapy. But he undermined every one of these efforts. His mistrust of his ability to assert control over his life became clear when he opted for a surgical procedure that would take responsibility for himself out of his hands once and for all.

Though he said he wanted to take control over his life, he sabotaged this as soon as he found a way of obtaining the desired results without having to trust his own controls and initiatives.

The problem in working with individuals who are addicted lies in their ambivalence and confusion. Though the dynamics can be understood from a psychological perspective, the physiological aspects become involved, making them much more difficult to work with.

Chapter 7

The Repetition Compulsion

Isn't it easy to see when others are engaging in repetitious behavior? We see how their behavior is harming them or taking them around in circles. We may wonder: Why does she keep being attracted to the same type of mean-spirited man? Why are all of their children having the same difficulties? Why is he leaving his wife for yet another—who looks and acts, to us, a lot like the first, and second, and maybe even the third wife? We wonder, because we can see what is happening. Still, we are frequently blind to our own deeply ingrained patterns of repetition.

Why could that be? It is because the repetition compulsion has a number of characteristics, most important of which is that individuals suffering from it have little or no insight into what is causing their difficulties. Freud saw this as instinctual and, as such, virtually immune to modification. When working with people in the grips of a self-destructive compulsion, one sees how this behavior seems to be driven by uncontrollable forces. At times one feels that a hurricane is coming and all of the indications are that it is dangerous and threatening. But there is no way to stop it. Similarly, the repetition compulsion is a drive, a persistent, insistent, unstoppable, and inevitable force. The intellect is suspended, judgment is deferred, inhibition is cast to the winds. It is not too different from the drive that salmon have to swim upstream, lay eggs, and die. There are refrains one hears again and again such as, "*I know I should not rush into this marriage, but... I know I should delay having a child but... I know I shouldn't rush to divorce him but...*"

This behavior indeed seems to be "Beyond the Pleasure Principle," meaning that while for most of us, human behavior is motivated by a desire for pleasure, for those caught up in this compulsion, even the instinct for pleasure is subverted to the need to repeat.

The repetitive games that children play are driven by pleasure seeking, by attempting to gain a sense of mastery. But the mastery of "peek-a-boo" or "hide-and-seek" may also represent attempts to gain mastery over fears or traumatic experiences such as fears of separation and abandonment. Some forms of seeking pleasure are self-destructive and dangerous, games that have anything but pleasurable consequences. But here too, the goal may be to prove mastery, albeit to the point of grandiosity, by defying the odds, by defying nature, by attempting to cheat death. Often dismissed as "masochistic behavior" we know that the dynamics are deep-seated and complicated.

What are the motives and the consequences of this compulsion to repeat that has self-punishing consequences? Is the person engaging in an activity to prove something to himself, or is he doing it to act out toward or against others? Is it inner-personal or interpersonal? Race car driving, rock and mountain climbing, downhill ski racing are examples of activities where the motive is to prove that one can gain mastery by engaging in dangerous and death-defying activities, that one can win against tremendous odds, that one can pit himself against nature itself. Such activities are motivated by attempts to prove mastery to one's self. Sometimes something goes seriously wrong, and it may involve others. But the motive is not to hurt others.

One cannot deny that great things come from some forms of behavior that require grueling training and punishment to the body. The Olympic Gold Medal winner goes through years of torturous training and, often, multiple accidents before becoming a winner. The ballerina goes through painful exercises in order to dance for little financial gain. The challenge is to achieve the hoped-for goal that is elusive and exceedingly challenging and difficult. But, for the most part, such efforts are defined by the individual who is aware of the price that has to be paid. He or she chooses to pay it for personal joy, gratification, and rewards.

However, when such punishing behavior involves others, involves placing them at risk, then the motives and goals have to be questioned. The predictable consequences are more likely to be in the service of not only hurting one's self, but of hurting others. The purpose is to repeat one's needs to abuse or to be abused, to gain revenge, to please others at one's own expense, or to repeat hurts by reenacting them through relationships.

That's how it is with repetitions. We may experience a sense of deja vu, when relationships repeatedly don't work out or when we run into the same kind of trouble with one job after another. Yet we rarely recognize the deep-rooted basis of our own repetitions, let alone take the emotional steps needed to change them.

What motivates people to repeat behavior that is at odds with their happiness, fulfillment, survival, or other sensible goals? Freud thought he had figured this out through his work with traumatized World War I veterans who reenacted and dreamed of their terrible war experiences. His work with them led him to the notion of the Repetition Compulsion—an instinct toward death, thanatos. It was a controversial idea in his time, and has more or less fallen out of favor in ours.

The Death Instinct may be questionable, but the compulsion to repeat self-destructive actions is a notion that is too useful to discard. I have long been puzzled by this compulsion when I have encountered it in my patients and wondered what could be behind such behavior.

In my work, I see many kinds of repetitions. I see people who appear to be compelled to sabotage themselves, repeating gestures and actions that are self-mutilating and destructive. I see those who seem to have everything going for them, but who make themselves continually miserable, putting themselves and those close to them again and again into miserable situations. I am not speaking primarily of the suicidal gestures of a depressed person or the repetitive rituals of the obsessive compulsive (though these are part of the picture), but what seems to be a repetitive drive to harm the self and others to the point of no return. If humans are motivated by pleasure, as Freud said, good sex, good food, fun, comfort, etc., how can we explain the repetition of demonstrably self-destructive acts? How can we explain the repetition in dreams and memories of painful experiences? When we play out the same painful scenario time and again in real life, or in dreams, is it an attempt at mastery and control? Is it an attempt to change the outcome just for once? Or does the very act of repetition itself offer some peculiar gain, some inexorable drive?

Basic to the compulsion to repeat is an intense and intolerable anxiety. This state of intolerable anxiety is inevitably caused by the individual having experienced trauma, a subjectively terrifying experience that is thrust upon the self, causing one to feel helpless and out of control. The feeling is so overwhelming to one's psychological integrity, that the feelings are sometimes repressed, shut out from memory. In some cases, the entire event is forgotten. In other cases, the event is recalled, but the feelings associated with it are repressed. In some instances, the entire experience is recalled with such fear and loathing, that the individual overreacts to any event that may be remotely associated with the trauma. In any case, the trauma and the anxiety cannot simply be put to rest. Instead, one lives with the fear that the trauma will recur and, therefore, it must be relived in order to gain that illusory sense of mastery and control.

There is a fear, an expectation even, that the worst is inevitably going to happen. Living with this fearful expectation is so intense that, unconsciously, the urge is to make it happen, to precipitate it, in order to get it over with in order to relieve the anxiety. In other words, rather than live with the anxiety that bad things will surely happen at the hands of chance (of nature, of God) the individual takes matters into his or her own hands. It is almost as though one is determining: Rather than wait for the worst to happen when fate decides, I will make it happen in my own way and under my control. Thus I have a sense of mastery. The anxiety is relieved, albeit, temporarily.

When Jack came to me, he was, from all outward appearances, an enviably successful man. A lawyer with his own practice, which he had founded with some partners, he had two children, a beautiful wife, and clear success. But as soon as he opened up to me, he revealed that he was engaged in a Russian roulette of close calls. He used his clients' escrow money to buy cars, Rolex watches, expensive vacations. When the escrow account came due, he scrambled around and plundered another account to pay it back. It was a game he knew he could not win and yet he seemed addicted to playing it. As our therapy progressed, I learned that his personal life was collapsing in on him as well. His wife—his second—had left him because he was carrying on an affair with his secretary, another in a long line.

One of the first things Jack said to me was this: "I don't really believe anybody can help me. Only I can help myself. I'm afraid to expose myself or reach out for help. I have to free myself of people I feel close to, indebted to, obligated to. I don't want to feel owned by anybody." And yet he had come for therapy.

Lots of people resist therapy even if they initially seem cooperative and willing to work through their problems in a therapeutic setting. Jack, however, was a world-class resister. He arrived for his first appointment ten minutes late, and I soon learned that this would be one of his patterns. He looked brusquely around my office, then having surveyed the room which was not, I could tell from his demeanor, up to his high standards, plopped down on the chair opposite me with a rather disdainful look.

It soon became clear that he had entered therapy grudgingly and only when his wife, Tracy, threatened to divorce him. They were already separated, and he was ambivalent about returning home, not the least because his wife had a deep well of anger at him.

Still, the idea that he needed therapy was not completely alien to him. He sensed that things were wrong with him, that he was on a bad road, and that people were getting fed up with him. Not only his wife. His colleagues had warned him to slow down, told him that he was "skating on thin ice," possibly destroying the very firm which he had worked so hard to build. Jack was feeling increasingly trapped and isolated.

Jack grew up with a nagging, demanding mother. "I manipulate others as my mother manipulated my father and me. I tried to please her by being a good kid, by overachieving."

To combat this, he now resorted to the same blind, passive-aggressive defenses he used with his mother. He could not even admit to himself that his mother was difficult, let alone confront her.

Jack was on a rollercoaster of grandiosity, but when I met him, most of the thrills were behind him and even he was beginning to realize that he was reaching the end of the line. Still, despite that realization, he could not seem to stop himself. Like a compulsive gambler, he somehow thought he could beat the odds.

From a clinical standpoint, these deep-seated, instinctual, often grandiose repetitions are usually the most frustrating. Insight alone is insufficient. Often, such patients are intelligent and articulate enough to give lip service to recognizing their unhealthy patterns.

Jack certainly was. "I get people committed to me and then I let them down," he admitted. "I can't stay committed because I'm afraid of failure." During the course of therapy, he spoke of terrible fears of being consumed by women, of a quasi-sexual relationship with his mother, and the fact that nothing terrified him more than being like his weak, impotent father whom his mother had humiliated virtually into nonexistence in the family.

He could say all these things, acknowledge them intellectually, but he could not emotionally open up enough to truly enter the therapeutic alliance. He had never experienced a relationship that was open and trusting, let alone one where both parties were equal. And so, he had nothing to base one on now. Instead, he cast me in the role of an agent of society's expectations, aligned with his wife, trying to bring him to heel. He resisted every step of the way, showing up late to appointments, skipping the next session with no notice just when it seemed as if we were getting somewhere, playing all sorts of games to maintain his sense of superiority to the therapeutic process.

For such individuals, something fundamental needs to shift in the course of therapy. Therapeutic relationship, as already noted, carries with it many of the distortions and overtones of relationships from the past. In fact, the therapeutic relationship is based largely upon the tendency to repeat early significant relationships. The therapist, being a human being, may tend to transfer onto the patient some of his or her own distortions from the past. However, when this occurs, it is to be hoped that the therapist is aware that this is happening. It is hoped that the therapist can use this reaction as a barometer of what is taking place in the therapeutic interaction. In Jack's case, Jack viewed the relationship as competitive and adversarial, as a power struggle. Was this subject to revision? Could we establish an alliance that was nonthreatening? An emotional shift of seismic proportions was necessary.

Unfortunately, this was too much for Jack who, because of his history, was terrified of exposing any vulnerability or weakness. Because of this he had to maintain his distance, had to avoid commitment to the therapeutic relationship, a relationship that, by its very nature, implied that he could not handle everything himself.

"Who the hell are you?" he asked me, at one of our last sessions. "You're everybody and nobody. You're no smarter than I am. And I don't intend to be dependent on you so you can judge me."

Jack is a sad case for me, a "failure" it might seem. His was such a classic case of pervasive repetitions. His self-destructive behavior permeated every aspect of his existence, and eventually destroyed a large part of it. He eventually lost his business, as well as his wife and children. Nothing, it seemed, had been able to stop his downward spiral.

Jack's behavior was an example of a different way of looking at Freud's Death Instinct. As a reaction to his fear of being destroyed, of losing hold of his fragile sense of identity, he, and others like him, become engaged in a doomed battle to control death, to bring it about on his own terms. Basically, as I see it, the inevitable is death and the repetition is to cheat death—only to discover that it cannot be cheated. Jack felt castrated because of his early life's experiences. Psychologically, castration and death are the same. He was intent on proving that he could not be vanquished and that he could conquer death. In one way or another, he and others like him are attempting to control something that is beyond anyone's control. They bring about the conclusion which they see as inevitable anyway—disgrace, ruin, even death, but on their terms. This is "beyond the pleasure principle."

Jack also illustrates the limitations of insight in resolving deeply ingrained self-sabotaging behavior. While insight *is* certainly a first step in the course of dynamic psychotherapy, the intellectual awareness must be translated into changes in feelings, in self-perception, and in behavior for significant restructuring to take place.

One can only envision Jack as Sisyphus, trying repeatedly to push the boulder uphill, only to watch it roll back down, and once again heave his shoulder beneath it and once again begin the futile journey uphill. It could break one's heart.

Unlike Jack, Cy's repetition compulsion seemed not to affect his corporate life. There, he was successful and admired. It was only in his home life and his intimate relationships that things were in turmoil.

Cy was fiftyish, one of those lucky people who was aging gracefully, at least on a physical level. He was trim and tall, with strong regular features and wavy salt-and-pepper hair. He cut an appealing figure when he first walked into my office and I immediately found him likeable. Looking closer, I noticed that the corners of his mouth turned down slightly, and he had the aura of sadness that I have come to recognize in so many of my patients. Once we settled in, I asked him what had brought him here, and he got right to the point. "I'm here because of my wife. She insisted that we both need therapy. You see, we haven't been sexually intimate in a long time, and she blames me for that. I think she's getting ready to leave me. I guess she's right. It is my fault."

I wondered immediately about Cy's willingness to take blame for something that, after all, was probably born out of the complicated dance that is marriage.

"Why do you think it's your fault?" I asked.

"I just don't desire her that way anymore. I lost it somewhere along the way," he said, looking between his folded hands. His body language was becoming increasingly inward, and I could tell that despite his efforts to be open, it was painful for him to talk about his intimate life. "The few times I've tried, I lost my erection. She tried to be understanding about it, at first, but I just can't take that. I feel like why bother if I just know I'm going to fail. Lately, she's been getting very hostile which just makes me want to avoid the whole thing."

He paused, so I asked him what he meant by *the whole thing*.

"Oh, I've been staying at work late. One night I didn't come home at all. I know I'm not being a good husband, but I just can't take her anger all the time. She's seething at me. Everything she says is clipped, or sarcastic, or critical. I don't think it's very good for our child to see their mother treating me like that."

"You have a child?"

"Yeah, he's just two. But I'm sure he picks up on the atmosphere."

"Well, having a toddler can often be hard on a marriage. How were things before you became parents?"

"Things were great. The sex was great. I never had a problem in that department. She was a very attractive woman. She *is* a very attractive woman. She took her pregnancy weight right off, or most of it. Sure, we had some fights, but nothing like this. We both wanted the same things. We were looking forward to starting a family. She's younger than I am. I have children from my previous marriage, but I agreed to be a father again, and she really wanted to have a baby. It seemed like a good marriage, much better than my first one. I loved—make that *love*—my wife. I love my kid. I don't know what happened. I feel awful."

I had a lot of questions, but I didn't want to rush Cy. Whenever I have a patient whose second marriage is in trouble, I naturally want to know what happened in the first marriage, and whether any of the same patterns that led to its dissolution are in play again. They almost always are. People tend to select similar mates, and reenact similar dramas in serial marriages. But for this first session, Cy needed the chance to get some things off his chest, and he needed to talk to someone who was not judging him, although he did plenty of that himself. He oscillated between anger at his wife and blame for himself. He had obviously expended a lot of energy keeping his anguish to himself, and I thought he left the office looking just a little bit lighter just for having talked. Before he left, we set up a weekly schedule—I would have preferred to see him more—but he said his busy schedule at work prevented it.

Meanwhile, my wife, who is also a psychotherapist, was having her first consultation with Cy's wife, Judy. The fact that Cy and his wife could both receive individual therapy under the single roof of our office had made it that much easier for them to seek help in the first place. That way from time to time the four of us might all meet to discuss things, an appealing prospect, but those four-way meetings needed to be carefully timed. My wife and I have worked with other couples in a similar fashion, designing a plan of action that suits their needs. Cy and his wife each wanted individual therapy, and I agreed. Given the painful nature of Cy's complaint, and his evident anger with his wife, I thought he needed to get a handle on his own emotions before he could benefit from couples therapy.

"I never thought I would be impotent," Cy began, the following week. "I don't know what's wrong."

"Is this the first time you've ever had this problem?" I asked.

"Well, no, to be honest. I had some problems with sexual performance in my first marriage. Not at first, but after a while. Maybe that's just the nature of the male beast—or my nature, anyway—we lose interest after a while."

"Tell me about what happened during that time."

"There's not that much to tell. I stopped lusting after her as well, after a while, and she got fed up with me and divorced me. I guess women are not very tolerant of husbands who don't perform. She was very wrapped up with the baby, and I was under some stress at work, and I didn't feel like coming home just to be snapped at after working hard all day to support our family. She said I was avoiding her and our child, that I didn't love them, which is wrong. I loved my wife and kids."

He paused, and I decided not to fill up the silence with any questions. Frequently in the course of a session, unlike a normal conversation, it is best to leave the awkward silence there for the patient to fill. It may be that they'll dig deeper, or ask themselves what it is that they are trying to avoid looking into.

"I just don't find pregnant women sexually attractive," Cy blurted out. "I mean, is that so damn unusual? Am I the only man who feels that way? I admit it, when Judy got pregnant, I didn't want to have sex with her anymore. Her body wasn't the same one I married. I'm not blaming her. It wasn't her fault. I'm just not attracted to fat women. I mean I know she wasn't really fat, but you know what I mean. I was afraid of hurting her or the baby. I thought she was in a fragile state. I admit it—I was surprised when she would express interest in having sex. I thought it was a little inappropriate."

He paused. I sensed he was looking for some sort of male camaraderie or approbation from me in this moment. I was formulating a response and wanted to be careful. Of course, I've given this subject a great deal of thought. The transformation of a love object/sexual and romantic partner into a mother, and one's own transformation into a father is fraught with sexual implications, which can ripple through the best of marriages and leave damaged and hurt feelings in their wake.

I'm well aware that sexual desire can fluctuate. Sometimes it goes downhill as soon as a couple marries. Pregnancy, the changes a woman's body goes through, and babies shake a lot of things up, including sex lives. The commitment of marriage and the commitment of fatherhood are momentous things for a man and can resonate in his sexual appetite.

Time was running out in what had turned out to be a very revealing session. It was becoming clearer to me that some of the same forces which had wrecked Cy's first marriage had brought the second to the brink as well. Both went south once the wives became pregnant and they never really recovered. Cy even expressed relief when he talked about his first wife's initiating divorce proceedings. He had wanted out, but he hadn't wanted to be the bad guy, the one who abandoned his wife and child. He claimed he had loved his wife and had never wanted to hurt her, but had waged a kind of passive-aggressive campaign that he claimed to be unaware of, to alienate her, avoid her, and push her away. He admitted that in the first marriage, after the baby was born, he sometimes deliberately stayed away from home or would "forget" to call to let his wife know where he was. He would do other things which he knew, on some level, would irritate her, sometimes running up debts on their jointly held credit cards behind her back, only to trigger an explosion when the bill came due.

At times, I admit, I would lose track of which marriage Cy was discussing, the dynamics of their unraveling were so similar. The only difference was that Judy, his current wife, unlike Celeste, his first, seemed determined not to let him off the hook so easily. She wanted to make him confront his behavior and deal head-on with the problem. And, despite the fact that he had agreed to go to therapy and was giving lip service to wanting to save the marriage, he seemed almost equally determined to avoid confronting the issue. When we zeroed in on the fact that pregnancy had been the trigger that led to trouble in each of the marriages, he backed off that line of inquiry abruptly.

"I'll tell you, I love my kid, but sometimes I think it would be better for everyone if Judy and I just went our separate ways." It was his way of signaling that he had gone deep enough. "I just wish we didn't have all these problems," he muttered. Cy often used generalities and self-pity as defenses when the going got a little rough.

I wanted to end the session on a resonant note, to give Cy something to mull over in the coming week, so that we could pick up where we left off in what was obviously beginning to be fruitful territory.

"What I'm hearing you say, Cy, is that your marriages, both your marriages, were pretty good before your wives became pregnant, before they became mothers. It might be good to explore some of your feelings about your own mother."

He stood to go. "My mother is a wonderful woman," he fired back.

Cy missed our next session. And I would soon discover that this form of passive-aggressive resistance would be a pattern with him as well. When he returned the following week, he nearly fell over himself apologizing. He had, he said, inadvertently scheduled an important meeting with a client at the same time as our session. "I double-booked myself," he said. "Didn't realize it until it was too late. I'm really sorry. Actually, my secretary should have caught the mistake, but she didn't. It's so hard to find good help these days."

It never occurred to him, or if it did, he refused to acknowledge it, that he was unconsciously sabotaging the therapy, just as it threatened to move into territory that made him profoundly uncomfortable. He stayed firm in the belief that he was in control of his actions, and that if things went wrong then it had to either be someone's fault or a completely innocent mistake.

"Boy, it's been so long, I can't even remember what we were talking about," Cy said. "My shortcomings as a husband, probably. I've been hearing a lot about that lately."

"As I recall, we were going to explore some of your feelings about your mother."

"Oh, great," he said. "You must have been talking to my wife. She thinks I have some mommy fixation, or something. She keeps insisting that there's something wrong with me."

I decided not to rise to the bait.

"I've really put some distance between my mother and me. I call her much less often. I've hurt her, probably very deeply. Does Judy appreciate this? No."

"I'm not sure what you mean."

"Well, let's see. Oh, I guess Judy's right. Maybe I was too close with my mother. I never rebelled. She was all alone, you know, after my father left. And he dragged it out, too. He kept leaving and coming back, and getting our hopes up, until he left for good. It was tough on all of us. I never wanted my mom to feel abandoned like that again, so, you know, I felt like that's what Judy's asking me to do. Abandon my mother again."

"What were things like for you after your father left?"

"I just got really careful and nervous. I started stuttering, felt like everyone was staring at me all the time. I also couldn't stop worrying about my mom, so I never got into trouble. If I went out, which was rare, I always told her where I was going, and who I was with. I never stayed out late. I was a really good kid, the kind of kid every mother wants. When other kids started smoking and drinking, or smoking pot, I always left. I didn't want to disappoint my mother again. And I was sure that if I did, something terrible would happen to me. On the few occasions when I did get a little high or drunk, later on in college, it wasn't even worth it because I felt so guilty about what it would do to my mom if she found out. She had very high standards for her kids. She was a pretty classy lady herself. And she needed me. I was, you know, pretty much the man of the house once Dad left."

"Did your mother appreciate all of your efforts?"

"I guess she did. You know, she had her own worries. She told me she had all she could handle and that I should always be a good boy or it would just put her over the edge and how would I like that to happen? But no matter how good I was or how much I tried to please her, I always felt like she favored my brother. He got away with murder."

"That must have hurt you."

"No, not really. She was a great mother. She had her own troubles. I feel terrible for having hurt her. But, Judy insists that we see less of her."

In the course of our sessions, and in some joint sessions we held with his wife, it became clear that Cy's acquiescent behavior toward his mother was reenacted with his wife and there was a similar undercurrent of resentment in both relationships. Cy was a successful man in the corporate world, but at home in his intimate relationships he was strangely unassertive. When Judy criticized him or complained about him, he became extremely defensive, and reflexively denied that he would ever do anything to hurt her. Though it was clear that he was angry with his wife, he could not, even within the relatively safe parameters of therapy, ever address that anger.

The full extent of Cy's passive-aggressive behavior in his marriage soon showed itself. He came to a session several months into his therapy announcing that Judy was so fed up with him that she was ready to divorce him. He didn't seem that upset about this prospect; in fact, he seemed relieved. What had happened was this:

For months, Cy had been staying at work late, in part, he had already admitted, to avoid coming home in order to dodge Judy's sharp tongue. Sometimes, in the later hours of the evening at the office, he contacted women over the Internet just to chat, he said, just to have some interaction with the opposite sex that wasn't filled with the hostility he had come to associate with his marriage. Once or twice he had even met these women for lunch. "Nothing sexual ever happened," he insisted, and I had no reason not to believe him. "I have no sexual desire for other women. Anyway, I'm impotent, so I couldn't cheat on Judy even if I wanted to."

Of course, Judy had found out about these liaisons; Cy had not gone to great lengths to hide them. She refused to believe they were innocent, and was certain Cy was cheating on her. She lambasted him for not being man enough to tell her and for sneaking around. There had been a terrible scene, complete with thrown plates and threats. Cy was sure that Judy was serious about divorcing him this time and just as certain that it was all his fault.

It was obvious that Cy felt that by finally revealing his "misdeeds" to me that he was doing exactly what the therapeutic relationship required, being totally honest and admitting his own "guilt," in the hopes of some sort of absolution. But therapy is not like confession, a place where one comes to be absolved of one's sins, and at any rate, there's no such thing as a sinner in psychotherapy. But Cy's tendency to blame himself, to blame others, and to seek absolution, underlined the judgmental nature of his background and orientation. Someone had to be at fault; someone had to be guilty and pay a price.

Though I liked him and found him personable, Cy had turned into an extremely frustrating patient. I felt that I could not get through to him and that his pattern was to resort to blaming himself as a defense, as if he were giving me a hot potato, hoping I'd drop it. But he simply would not dig deeper into his feelings. He remained extremely guarded even when he was convinced he was being perfectly honest. For example, though it was obvious in everything he said, Cy had a hard time admitting that he was angry with his wife. Even more remote was the possibility of getting him to own up to feeling any anger at his mother, let alone to see the connection that this formative relationship might have to his present circumstances.

Cy had never gained the ability to express his anger directly at the people who caused it—that is, his needy mother, from whom he could never gain favored-child status, and his abandoning, severely critical, and irresponsible father. Instead his anger was camouflaged and expressed deviously, in such a way as to get revenge while simultaneously hurting himself. Cy had wanted to avoid becoming his father—a man who abandoned his family. Cy had to become "not his father" by pleasing his mother. He was failing miserably on both counts. He was on the verge of effectively abandoning his second wife and child, and though he had various rationalizations for this, it was clearly eating him up inside. He had never really effectively separated from his mother and had de facto become the man in her life when his father left, an unhealthy situation fraught with oedipal dangers for everyone concerned.

The pivotal point in both of his marriages, I had tried to point out to him, was when his wives became pregnant: pregnancy equals motherhood equals his wife equals his mother. Therefore, sex is forbidden. His wives' pregnancies also meant a transformation of his status to that of father, another problematic state. Fathers, in his deepest-felt experience, abandon their children, a terrible thing in his mind. Although being such a father was a profound fear of his, he was also driven to repeat the traumatic experience that he underwent. Fatherhood was a terrible risk in the light of Cy's abandonment by his father. After all, as a young child, he idolized his father only to get mocked and degraded by him. Cy tried to please his father, but his efforts were always met with failure. Cy became disillusioned with his father, but more important, with himself. He felt that he was a failure, which was the message that he received from his father.

Then there was the matter of his impotency, an apparently physical symptom, which is where all of Cy's problems converged. If he's impotent, he cannot have sex with his wife/mother. He also cannot be a father to a child he will eventually abandon. (How could he impregnate his wife if he is impotent?) His impotence also has the effect of making his wife feel undesirable, creating alienation in the marriage, and an eventual out for him. Meanwhile, he can toy with meeting other women, further upsetting his wife while simultaneously assuring himself that he will not have sex with them. He is impotent, after all. Looked at objectively, and without regard to any of the hurt feelings generated all around, his impotence, as a strategy of his unconscious, was quite perversely ingenious. Eventually, presumably, if the script continued as it was, he would be free of this entanglement, and free to start the whole cycle again.

I wish I could tell you that my delicate hinting at some of these deeper connections and causes of Cy's behavior had a palliative effect. But that seemed not to be the result. Rather, things seemed to be moving swiftly toward a divorce. I tried telling Cy that I thought he needed to give careful consideration to how it was that he was finding himself in a very familiar place. I reminded him that divorce was not the issue with which he needed to come to terms. Rather it was the underlying dynamics of why he kept himself in the same situation. Further, I made clear my sense that his drive to end his marriage was too intense, too driven. I told him that perhaps I could understand his drive to leave if he had another woman whom he craved, but that was not the case.

Things between Cy and his wife staggered forward. My relationship with Cy also seemed very rocky.

I try never to give up on a patient, and joyfully, my dealings with Cy confirmed that there is always hope. He came to one session after having seen a movie that referred to masturbation as normal adolescent behavior.

"I never masturbated when I was a teenager," he said. "I wonder why. I guess I was afraid I'd get caught. Afraid I'd be ashamed."

This opened up a host of memories of remarks Cy's mother had made when he was a teenager about his father's "disgusting" sexual behavior and the "disgusting" sexual behavior of men in general. Yet, Cy recalled that his mother frequently walked around in front of him in various states of undress including in the nude. At the time, he thought nothing of it. But now he wondered why she had done it. He also remembered that his mother had bought him clothes that were at odds with the mores of young adolescents in his day, clothes that other youngsters considered "sissy" clothes. Revealing these things, Cy suddenly felt the need to assure me that he was not gay and had no interest in men sexually. But he became aware of the painfully contradictory messages he had received from his mother, and realized that he had become accustomed to repressing the sexual feelings that were aroused by her.

And so it was, that because of all the groundwork that we had done, that Cy was ready for the emergence of these memories and feelings when he saw the movie. The work we had done prepared him for the realization of how repressed he had been. His mother negated his sexuality while stimulating him to admire and react to her sexually.

Following the emergence of these memories and his emotional reactions to them, Cy felt sexual desire for his wife for the first time in years. For the first time in years, they had successful intercourse.

The Oedipus complex is the basis of many jokes about psychoanalytic theory and is often dismissed out of hand. However, when one faces the many ramifications of oedipal issues in one's own analysis and in the analysis of patients, it is no joke. It is central and crucial to many difficulties throughout life and marriage and child rearing.

In Cy's case, it was especially relevant. His mother was seductive walking around in the nude in front of him. This has to be stimulating to a young boy. But what does he do with this stimulation? Cy had no choice but to repress his feelings in order not to react to this overwhelming and premature sexual stimulation from the forbidden sexual object in the form of mother. This process of repression of sexual feelings not only took place in childhood and adolescence, but also recurred with his wives when they became pregnant. Pregnant women were mothers-to-be and sex was out of question. Indeed, all sexual urges had to be denied and repressed, even at the expense of his own feelings of adequacy. To make matters worse, his father failed to serve as a consistent, loving force in his life. He failed to provide the protection the boy needed to control his sexual urges. His mother, while stimulating him, also denigrated male sexuality and masturbatory urges which would have provided him with an outlet and some modicum of assurance about his masculinity. Instead, his mother attempted to dress him as an asexual or even feminine adolescent. Of course, her favoring Cy's brother as "the male" and Cy as the "good little boy" only made matters worse.

Cy's efforts to distance himself from his mother, largely at the behest of his wife, had done little to resolve his conflict because his wife had already taken the mother's place in his psyche. Her pregnancy reawakened the need to renounce the mother as a sexual object as had been the case in his previous marriage. Cy really did not have an adequate male identification figure in his life to provide him with direction. His inconsistent and critical father abandoned him and he had hated him for it. His father had resorted to passive-aggressive ways of dealing with his family, coming and going and gaining revenge on his wife by avoiding and escaping issues. Cy was repeating this by staying out nights and resorting to guilt-filled self-recriminations. To him, it was inevitable that he, like his father, was fated to leave his wife and child. Divorce and abandonment had to happen. So the feeling was that it was best to get it over with. As Freud and his followers pointed out, the male Oedipus complex cannot be successfully resolved without identification with the father.

The resolution of this problem through psychotherapy was for Cy to utilize his relationship with the analyst to work through this problem. Cy fought this by missing sessions, by being late, and by spending much time resisting in the form of blaming and judging himself and his wife. This was his self-sabotaging maneuvering aimed at the status quo. Change came hard. It meant confronting feelings that were distasteful and risking turning his world, as unpleasant as it was, upside down. Change takes place through the therapeutic relationship and it was difficult for Cy to fully commit to this.

However, gradually, Cy became more open and direct in his communications. He was still overly defensive, but everything began to change. The focus of his dreams, which early in therapy had to do with plane crashes and tragedies that could not be avoided, changed to dreams about his father, who had not been a focal point up to now. Cy had not seen his father for years and still had no desire to see him. But his associations to his father and that relationship opened strong feelings of pain and suffering with recollections of his father's abusive treatment. Cy's anger at his father became more openly expressed, along with sadness that he never really had a supportive father and was left to make up for the damage his father did to him and his mother.

The emergence of these dreams suggested that Cy was ready to move on, to realize himself and his own needs and desires. Relations with his wife improved, their sex life became reawakened, and he was better able to take charge of his own life and to show the initiatives that had been absent. He no longer resorted to passive-aggressive maneuvering, but was more open and direct. Cy changed and his relationships with himself and his family changed as well. And so this, one of the most difficult kinds of repetitive behavior, was finally tamed, and Cy was, for the most part, free.

The downward spiral in Cy's marriage and his sabotaging behavior was prompted by another important consideration. Referred to as "The Anniversary Reaction," he was unconsciously propelled to terminate his marriage after the same number of years that his parents' marriage lasted. This emerged when he was at his wit's end and was ready to seek a divorce. He said, "I know I destroyed my marriage and I have to live with this." This led in turn to the realization that he was acting like a robot in his destructive behavior in the form of terminating his marriage. He had not had any awareness that in the recesses of his mind was the belief that his marriage would not, could not, last longer than that of his parents. It was as though he were programmed to bring the marriage to an end after the same number of years. This served as an epiphany, opening doors to a greater awareness that his behavior was beyond his control and outside his consciousness.

Anniversary reactions are seen in many forms. When the anniversary reactions are not conscious, depressive moods may overwhelm an individual inexplicably, and it is only later that one realizes that on that given date a parent died, an abortion took place, or some other significant happening had occurred.

Many religions ritualize anniversaries based upon a deep-seated appreciation of the human tendency to keep an accounting of significant events in life. They make a ritual of marking time, of making certain that the anniversary is conscious and out in the open. Whether it be the Yahrzeit in the Jewish religion or the Memorial Mass in Catholicism, there is recognition that a significant event took place on such and such a date. It represents a way of marking that event. Without such awareness many people "forget" or "don't know" the date, only to react in a variety of ways with a variety of feelings that they cannot explain. In Cy's case, the realization that he was marking the time of his marriage based upon the longevity of his parents' marriage was an epiphany that articulated clearly that he was destroying his marriage by a hidden force that dictated how long his marriage should last and when it should end.

The "anniversary reaction" is a good example of the repetition compulsion at work. The trauma of divorce, loss, death is repressed but reenacted through behavior in the form of mood swings or prompting actions that cannot be explained.

In earlier chapters we discussed Howard and Arthur, two men who were aggressive and abrasive in ways that created difficulties on their jobs and in their personal lives. This was true for Jack, as well.

Max was a different story. Max was unable to work consistently. He became blocked and paralyzed. Much of his work required him to write copy. He was engaged in a not-for-profit venture aimed at improving the environment, but it involved butting-up against strong political forces on the side of big business. He wanted to help the world but he didn't bargain for the need to fight aggressively in order to achieve his goals. Max was afraid of his own aggression and was fearful of retaliation if he succeeded.

Max described his mother as ferocious. She was negative about everyone and everything. Max was born during the Second World War while his father was overseas. He didn't see his father until he was three or four years old. During those early years, his mother was furious at his father for being away. To her, it was as though the father had abandoned his family. She seemed to care not at all that a war was on and her husband had been drafted. When his father finally did come home, mother continued to vent her rage at him for leaving. To make matters worse, his father brought home war stories describing occasions in which he was shot at while scouting out the enemy. Though he was not hurt, he spoke of acting aggressively in doing his job. This only made his mother more anxious and more angry at the realization that he really could have gotten killed and she would have been left alone with a child.

The message came through clearly. If you act aggressively, retaliation is sure to follow. People will kill you or your wife will be angry with you. Max's resolution was to be the good guy, to help others, to help the world, and not to be aggressive. He avoided getting into fights or arguments throughout his schooling or college. He did what was expected of him and maintained distance from others. He entered into environmental protection activities that took him to distant parts of Asia and Africa, always on the side of doing what he viewed as the right thing. And always at low rates of compensation. He preferred to stay behind the scenes, not in the forefront. He did his job and others got the credit and that was just fine with him. Until—he got involved in a project that brought him into direct opposition with powerful business forces that fought his efforts. At this point, he could not work. Preoccupied with the fact that he was blocked and could not write the copy that was required of him, he was unaware of what might be getting in the way. He knew he was anxious, but he thought he was anxious because he couldn't work.

In the course of therapy, largely through his dreams of being attacked by large frightening animals, it emerged that he saw himself as the one who was being destroyed. He blocked because he viewed his writing as an aggressive act that could only bring him trouble and pain for doing what he believed in. (It's interesting that Max eschewed work that could have compensated him far better if he were able to put himself on the line and act more assertively. Instead, he played it safe by working in a field that paid far less and that was fostering a positive social cause.) To his amazement and alarm though, he discovered that his choice of the "safe way" turned out to be not so safe. Just as his father was serving his country only to incur the wrath of his wife, so Max was serving his cause only to live in fear of being seen as the enemy—at least, to the opposition.

Where others see themselves as fighters, to demonstrate that they can withstand the opposition and vanquish it, Max avoided confrontation and fighting. He lived under a cloud that dictated that good must be followed by bad, success must be followed by failure. This was clearly demonstrated when Max had to give a presentation before a significant group whose support he needed badly. He worked under tremendous pressure to prepare this presentation. It was successful and achieved the results that he had hoped for. When he spoke about this, he was insistent that something had to happen to undermine his success. He could not allow himself to feel good about his accomplishment, but had to prepare himself for the worst. Clearly, Max suffered from anhedonia and pleasure defects. He suffered from overwhelming and ubiquitous guilt feelings that were related to feeling undeserving.

Another aspect of the tendency to repeat is based upon a person's self-image. We structure and interpret our world within the framework of the way in which we see that world and ourselves within it. A person who has grown up feeling that he is capable and effective will view his world quite differently from the one who feels incapable and ineffective. One's confidence in one's ability to cope with the world will be reflected in the way one structures relationships. One who has friends, who feels confident and attractive, will relate differently than one who feels stupid, weak, or unattractive. This way of structuring one's world is involuntary[1] and automatic, part and parcel of one's personality. It is manifested in the people one associates with and the ways in which they relate. Do individuals tend to relate to others who are bullies? Or do they associate with others who carry themselves with self-respect and esteem? Are they the butt of jokes and mockery, relating to others who view them as fools, or are they respected and listened to? Do they view themselves as unworthy and undesirable, or as likeable and valuable? Do they, as parents, communicate to their children that they are downtrodden failures in an unfair world? Or do they demonstrate to their children that they are worthy and headed for a successful life? Are others out to take advantage of them, to misuse them so that they must be vigilant and on guard? Is the world a frightening place that is threatening them at every turn? Or is there a sense of security?

The difficulty is that such views of one's self occur subtly and early in life and usually permeate the atmosphere in the family. The cues and clues are communicated through parental attitudes toward themselves and toward others and even toward the world in general. These attitudes are accepted and internalized as "the way things are and there is nothing anyone can do about it." So the child continues to repeat the feelings and attitudes, the "Weltanschauung" that is part of the family structure. Those, like Fred, in Chapter 1, who are able to take a critical view of the belief system in the family run the risk of ostracism and rejection.

Helen was eleven years old when her mother brought her to me for treatment. As Helen and I worked together, I discovered these things: She was an only child, born to a family in which the father was a very successful workaholic, a man who was impatient with his wife and daughter. He could not tolerate error or imperfection and was highly critical of his wife and daughter. Mother tolerated his behavior. Helen did not. She aggressively confronted her father about his demeaning behavior toward her and her mother. Father became more abrasive. Helen's mother told Helen not to interfere and not to confront her father. Helen felt alone and without support from the person she was trying to help. She felt distant, alienated, and unable to express herself to either parent. She sought support from classmates but in a very needy way. Her sense of worthlessness permeated her life and she sought bolstering from almost everyone with whom she came in contact. Her neediness manifested itself in an awkward and inappropriately demanding manner. She tried to buy friends by imposing herself, by trying too hard to win favor.

Instead of attracting others, she repelled them by her neediness. Helen developed phobic reactions, which only made her life more difficult and made her stand out as strange and weird to others. We worked together for about six months and the situation at school and with peers improved somewhat. And then, before we could complete our work, the therapy was terminated by Helen's mother.

Helen returned to see me some thirty years later. She had completed college, traveled widely, and had had a short-lived marriage. However, her ways of relating to others remained the same as they were when she was just eleven years old. She tried to win friends by offering favors; she was gullible and naïve; she was an easy mark for others who took advantage of her because they sensed her intense neediness.

She continued to repeat again and again the same view of herself vis-a-vis the world and others. She structured her world in terms of the feeling that she was a reject, one whom others did not really like and did not want to associate with. She saw herself as undesirable and her task was to try to win others over, to force them to accept her. She was willing to pay a price to buy acceptance. Despite the fact that her efforts did not produce the desired results, she continued. She tried to win friends by ingratiating herself, by doing for them, by trying to please them in ways that were hugely inappropriate. She exposed herself as a person who was too needy for love and acceptance. Not only that, but in her efforts to appear friendly, enthusiastic, and exuberant, she communicated a sense that she was not authentic, that she was, in fact, phony, lonely, desperate. She sabotaged her chances to gain not only friendship, but also self-respect—because she communicated her true self-image as a hungry, needy individual who did not feel worthy of respect and caring.

When I first began working again with Helen after all those years, she had just moved into new living quarters. She wanted to meet her neighbors. She invited them to a party at her apartment. She planned on a party complete with servers to help, dinner, wine, flowers, etc. All of this was for people she did not even know. It caused her great consternation when I pointed out that she was repeating the same old theme again.

With some trepidation, she toned down her plans. Instead of an elaborate dinner, she invited neighbors for a small, informal cocktail party. Neighbors came, were thankful for the invitation, and seemed interested in establishing a neighborly friendship with her. She revealed to me that she was shocked to discover that she did not have to wine and dine others to enlist their friendship. She began to realize that her intense efforts were not only unnecessary, but also served to sabotage the very things she wanted.

But this awareness alone was not enough. Helen had to face the anger and frustration she had felt early in life, the pain of constant criticism, the sense that she was never good enough, that within her own family she could not get the security and reassurance she needed. She had to face her anger that in giving up seeking love from her family, she transferred her needs to others in her life, only to be spurned again.

It was a long, hard road with Helen. She did not want to admit to herself, much less to me, the anger she felt; she did not even allow herself to regret the rejections, the pain and sorrow she was experiencing. Instead, for a long time, she doggedly sought acceptance, continuing to overlook the fact that her efforts did not bring her what she needed and wanted. She placed herself repeatedly in situations in which she was being taken advantage of and misused. She made life difficult for herself to prove that she could survive all kinds of insults and threats.

At one point, she told how she got adrenaline rushes out of sky diving and bungee jumping to prove, she told me, that she was not afraid of life.

In fact, Helen was very much afraid of life. She felt vulnerable and at risk. Focusing only on her overt behavior did not and would not solve the problem. She had to deal with her underlying feelings.

In contrast to Helen, who lived with an image of herself as a "reject," there are others who see themselves as poor and deprived when, in fact, the objective reality is quite different. Such individuals have received most of the advantages and opportunities of middle or upper middle class, yet they view themselves as needy. They don't feel rejected, but they do feel *cheated*. For such individuals, the resulting feeling is one of entitlement, a sense that whatever they have gotten is not enough. This is repeated in a variety of settings and in many ways which always find expression in the form of—I must get something for nothing, without earning or working for it. I deserve it; I'm entitled to it. Sometimes the refrain goes like this: "What have you done for me lately? Or, I'll take what I want if you won't give it to me."

Sarah was a model. She was beautiful and well paid, working for a top modeling agency. She attended first rate private and boarding schools and then a respectable college. She was an only child whose parents were both busy professionals from the time she was born. She was raised by a variety of nannies who were good to her, but who came and left. Her parents doted on her and took pride in her looks and accomplishments, but gave little of themselves. Sarah had friends, play dates, and parties as a child, all of them accompanied by her nannies. Her parents had no time.

She grew up and married a handsome successful man who was very busy and traveled a great deal. Sarah came to therapy because she knew something was wrong with her behavior. She had everything, but she shoplifted. She had never—yet—been caught. She went to the finest clothing stores and managed to leave with additions to her wardrobe. She couldn't help herself. She did not feel guilty and she didn't even think about getting caught. She just had to do it. She knew she had a problem because she already had more than enough clothing and she could easily have purchased more. But the challenge, the compulsion, was to get something that she wanted without having to pay for it. She saw herself as "the poor little rich girl" who had everything, but yearned for more. She felt she was entitled to whatever she could get.

Like Helen, Sarah was starving, starving in a sea of plenty. She felt empty. Helen had to buy friends, had to get people to like her even if it meant forcing herself on them. Sarah had to get clothes for nothing even if it meant stealing them.

Both women experienced deep feelings of deprivation that they would not accept. They were both very angry and depressed, while presenting a façade of happiness. They both repressed their anger and sadness while repeatedly seeking the "cure" for their inner hungers. They persisted in trying to win love—to fill themselves up—in self-defeating ways.

The effect of sibling relationships on one's self-image and on life-long repetitions is important, because the ways in which we relate in later life are often determined by early interactions with siblings. Taunting and teasing, unfavorable comparisons with other siblings, the different ways in which siblings are treated within a family, all of these play an important role in the ways in which we see ourselves. Though sibling rivalry is generally considered normal and part of growing up within a family, there are extremes. These extremes are often traceable, not so much to the siblings, as they are to the way the parents relate to each other and to the children.

Competitive strivings, or alternately, avoidance of competition, can often be traced to sibling relationships. A child whose older sibling is rebellious and is punished by his parents may experience this as a clear signal not to rebel, to conform even if this means inhibiting feelings. The younger child becomes the "good kid" who never gets in trouble, conforming out of fear that the punishments meted out to the sibling can easily come his own way. Siblings can arouse feelings of guilty rage causing intense bitterness that can become part of the self-image, the way in which one sees one's self and others later in life.

But siblings can also be positive role models and sources of encouragement, especially in those instances in which parents work long hours or in single-parent families. Much depends on the parents.

Bertha, a forty-year-old depressed woman came for treatment because of chronic state of unhappiness, her inability to establish on-going relationships, difficulties in demonstrating affection for her children, and coldness in her marriage.

Following prolonged expressions of rage at her parents for failing to provide her with a more loving, warm environment, Bertha recalled an incident when she was four years old. Her mother told her to watch her baby sister outdoors while the baby was sleeping in her carriage. While she was carrying out this chore (which she did not enjoy), the carriage rolled off the sidewalk onto the road. The mother saw this out the window, ran out to retrieve the baby carriage and severely rebuked the four-year-old Bertha. This incident became a touchstone around which much of Bertha's life had been organized. As a result, partly of this incident in which she was given a burden much too severe for a four-year-old, she hated her sister. Her sister became the symbol of punishment and alienation from her mother. Bertha was intent on *not* being like her sister in any way. Her sister was a constant reminder of Bertha's ineptitude and the cause of difficulties with her mother.

As a result, Bertha reacted with hostility and negativism to demands made upon her, because she could not trust herself. She was fearful that her destructive urges might be translated into behavior—as happened when she was four. She could not let herself get too involved in caring for her own children and the responsibilities that went with her role as mother and caretaker.

Bertha's husband was a successful professional and was able to pay for help to ease the burden for Bertha. However, she was never satisfied with the help. The baby-sitters were never careful or attentive enough to the children. In fact, Bertha could not allow herself to feel happy about very much. She had to be constantly vigilant lest things get out of hand. Much of her behavior in adulthood was colored by her childhood relationship with her sister with whom she had little contact as an adult. However, her sister represented the person who made her whole life miserable.

In contrast to Bertha, Florence did not fight. Instead, she withdrew, sacrificing her own assertiveness. Florence was the oldest in a family of six children born to a mother who sacrificed her own educational and professional plans in order to have a family. The mother had very little patience with children, especially with her firstborn child, Florence. The mother didn't know what to do with her first child and she didn't take well to having her plans disrupted. In many ways, Florence had to grow herself because shortly following her birth, her mother became pregnant again and again and again. At first, as a small child, Florence tried to win her mother's affections by being her helper, by being a "mother surrogate" to the babies. She tried to take care of them, but she was too young and she could not succeed. Her mother became extremely impatient with her little helper. And the younger children wanted their mother's attentions, not their sister's. Florence gave up the fight for her place in the family by withdrawing and avoiding confrontations. She became the scholar, reading constantly and becoming a superior student—which only aroused the envy of the younger children.

Florence came to therapy following her entry into a new profession in which other women were bright, accomplished, and very competitive. Florence was just as bright and accomplished, but hardly competitive. She was well prepared in terms of knowledge, intelligence, and abilities, but she had trouble asserting herself. Where others advanced themselves to gain recognition in the field, Florence took a backseat. She saw colleagues move ahead, building major reputations. She was aware of their limitations, and more, she knew, correctly, that she could have done a much better job than they did. But this was all internal. She could not bring herself to put herself forward. She read and studied and worked at improving her knowledge and experience base. At meetings, however, though she had things to say, she deferred to others. She could not speak up.

Florence was reenacting her place in the family. Rather than fight, she withdrew and focused on self-improvement. In therapy, she realized what she was doing. She was feeling misplaced by her siblings who got most of mother's attentions. She realized, and she withdrew and was silent. She also realized that she now had a choice—she did not need to compete for recognition in the professional arena, or she could compete if she so wanted. But she could do it freely. She did not need to reenact what had been done to her in the past.

Chapter 8

Recognizing and Resolving
Self-Sabotaging Repetitions

Crucial to our understanding of the compulsion to repeat is the concept of trauma and the repression of feelings associated with trauma. In everyday language, we use the term "trauma" to refer to extrinsic happenings such as horrifying events that affect everyone exposed to them—events such as tornadoes, wars, tsunamis, or hurricanes. However, as used here, trauma refers to selective, personal experiences that shock and horrify, that undermine our basic assumption that our world has some stability. In other words, trauma here is defined by the way it is experienced by the individual, so that what is threatening and traumatic to one person may not be traumatic to another. For those who experience such traumatic events, there is a deep, compelling, unconscious need to gain control over what was experienced as being out of control. When we cannot gain this sense of control, we sometimes repress or bury our feelings and memories. Such repression is a way of protecting ourselves from experiences that overwhelm our emotional equilibrium, that were so awful we cannot keep them in our consciousness. But repression, as we have seen so clearly by now, does not bury the event alone, nor the feelings and memories attached to it. Rather it involves burying accompanying material along with it. The result is that such repressed memories and feelings are subject to a great deal of distortion.

There is a glut of recent literature[1] that deals with reactions of resilience and hardiness to trauma. Most of these studies are based upon short-term considerations and overt behavior. What is missing in many of these studies, however, is consideration of long-term effects of trauma on an individual, based upon that individual's history in experiencing trauma. Instead of talking about "hardiness," or "resilience" as entities in themselves, it is necessary to consider the full configuration of the life of a given individual. To be sure, there are individual differences, but sensitivities are diminished or exacerbated by life's experiences. It is also likely that biological and hereditary factors play a significant part when one speaks of "resilience" and "hardiness" in response to trauma. However, an individual who experienced trauma in childhood will react to later trauma quite differently from the person who has not experienced previous trauma. Essie would probably not have reacted to the 9/11 devastation as she did if she had not had the earlier experiences that she had.

For all victims of trauma, however, one distinguishing feature is the sense of loss of control. All of us, from early childhood on, need to feel that we have some control over ourselves and our lives. A child builds a tower of blocks. It falls. He rebuilds it. Children play hide-and-seek and peek-a-boo. It reassures them that what has disappeared has reappeared. And when these things work, the child feels pleasure, not only psychically, but also physiologically. All of this supports the development of a sense of constancy.

Sometimes, however, trauma and the repression that accompanies it, interferes with normal growth and this is where hopeless, self-defeating repetitive cycles can begin. When there are constant admonitions, punishment, rejection, manipulation, and criticism, a child's growth can be truncated. If the child expresses feelings or beliefs that are at odds with the parental proscriptions, when the price is disapproval, rejection, guilt, and the threat of abandonment, the child can be traumatized. Guilt is integral to the self-image. This can become a life-long repetitious pattern of suppressing and inhibiting one's assertiveness in order to please others.

Another extreme is also possible. Instead of suppressing and inhibiting one's assertiveness, the child can react in completely different ways. Stubborn defiance and resistance to the harsh and punitive parent can result in a chronic battle of wills aimed at proving that the individual will not be snuffed out by the parent. Authority must be challenged at every turn regardless of the consequences. *Beat me if you must, but I won't give you the satisfaction of seeing me cry.* Or the individual may defy others outside the home while behaving at home, an angel at home, but a devil with teachers in school, a bully on the playground toward other kids. In any case, he feels inadequate and ridden with guilt and self-recriminations. Eventually the child becomes the adult who challenges his wife or his boss. He displaces his angry feelings onto others who are perceived as treating him unjustly.

The basic conflict is based upon fears of rejection, loss of love, and ultimately, fears of annihilation. At the extreme, it is experienced as a life or death struggle to survive or to be destroyed.

The answer for such traumatized individuals, albeit a self-defeating one, lies in the lifelong need to master the trauma, to reassert control. I *will* be able to get my abusive parent to love me and to be good to me. I *will* be able to get my alcoholic parent to stop using alcohol. I can, I must, rescue them and rescue myself. I can get them to love me when they never did. I cannot fail—or *I will be a failure.*

There is, however, a variation on this theme. When anger at the disappointing parent is intense, when one feels there is no way to change the offending parent, the goal may become one of defiance—procrastination, avoidance, messiness, failure to fulfill promises, substance abuse. All of these represent passive-aggressive modes. Independence becomes equated with stubborn negativism and defiance.

Other traumatized individuals, in order to gain a sense of control, seek escape in a world of wish-fulfilling fantasies. The sex addict spends hours watching pornography, fantasizing a partner like those in the movie, a partner who will do anything to please him. Others use fantasy to gain revenge, taking pleasure in indulging in repetitive sado-masochistic fantasies. There, they feel they can ventilate their anger toward those who have insulted or wronged them—as they could not do in reality.

Others avoid fantasy, but instead doggedly attempt to right the wrongs despite the fact that they are unaware of what the wrongs were. They try, as did Helen, to win friends in awkward and self-defeating ways. Or, they try, as did Sarah, to get things for nothing—to shoplift—to compensate for feelings of being cheated. They may seek out conflict and confrontational situations like Jack, ultimately losing everything, or they may avoid such situations as did Max in his save-the-earth campaign.

The ultimate fear of loss of control is that of annihilation and death. In one form or another, much of what we do is aimed at proving that we can outwit the inevitable, a task which is beyond control and beyond reason. Man does not easily accept his own mortality and many of his compulsions and grandiose efforts are aimed at outwitting death.

And here, the hope to be able to rise to and overcome adversity— even to challenge death—is admirable if there is a realistic basis. The challenge of climbing Mt. Everest is fine if one is in top condition and climbs with an experienced guide. The need to become expert in a given field is admirable if one tempers it with realistic goals. But these are not the individuals of whom I speak here. Those who push limits to the ultimate, who disregard all dangers, end up in self-sabotaging patterns. One's own sense of omnipotence and grandiosity does not hold up. So these individuals try again and again to prove they can outwit the odds.

Because what does not change is the specter of death, the way we deal with that is significant. The way in which we confront our mortality is a determining factor in the way we live our lives. It has been said that man cannot conceive of his own death. This is our way of defending ourselves against what we know is out there, our mortality, our ultimate end. So to prove our immortality, we fight, we defend, we repeat our foibles.

How are such conflicts resolved? The answer is *not easily*. It's obvious by now that tuning into long-repressed painful memories and feelings arouses fears and anxieties over what will emerge and what the effects will be. After many years of protecting ourselves from our feelings, it is frightening to experience feelings that have been walled off; one will walk naked into the world.

What is going to be left of me if I let my feelings come forth?

I know I've been feeling depressed, but will I be far more depressed if I gain access to these feelings?

There's the rub. We go through life with our protective covering and we go through the motions of living. We get jobs, do our work, get married, and have children. Why stir the beast beneath? Why not just avoid and leave? Get divorced, quit the job, let the kids go, and justify it all in terms of bad breaks, a rotten boss, a bitchy wife, ungrateful children. It's easier to just go on, despite the real consequences, than it is to delve into causes of the tensions, frustrations, and disappointments.

The more one simply acts out, the less likely it is that he will look into himself. So we defend ourselves by repressing the memories and the feelings that go along with them. By repressing them, we think we forget them. But we don't because such feelings trigger rage and desires for revenge, or depression and disturbed thinking. Do such feelings go away so easily? Of course not. They are visited without our awareness upon our bosses, our wives, and our children. We become the abuser, the bully. We find revenge by becoming like the abusers, by victimizing others, or we prove that our tormentors were right.

"You'll never amount to anything" means "I can't let myself amount to anything and failure is my lot."

It's easier to act, to perpetuate self-sabotaging behavior than to come to grips with disappointments from the past. It's easier to live life as a robot than as a sentient, even depressed, human being. It's easier to fail or to withdraw, than it is to feel pain.

There are those who avoid this kind of pain and insight by being quick to blame themselves. *I know it's all my fault, I know I'm the guilty party, now leave me alone.* Under the guise of accepting blame, they free themselves of the need to come to grips with that which torments them.

The result is that one becomes an AS IF person.

If I become successful, it's a mistake.

If I get a promotion, I pulled the wool over my boss's eyes.

If my marriage is OK now, it won't be for long. I'm waiting for the ax to fall, waiting for them to catch on to me. I'm a phony, an imposter, a chameleon.

The dilemma is that if I am successful, my parents will be proud of me and I don't want them to have that satisfaction. But if I fail, it will prove that they were right. So I'm left in a bind. I lose either way—that is, if my goal is to gain revenge against my parents, there is no me. I am only a robot reacting to the programmed commands of my frustrating parents, to prove them right or wrong, to please them or disappoint them. This state of detachment becomes internalized into a state where one is inauthentic. One develops a façade, a "false self,"[2] a mask of presenting one's self as if she were someone other than who she really is. *I am not acceptable as I am so I must act as if I am someone I think I ought to be.*

Such an individual may present himself as strong or weak, glamorous or earthy, sophisticated or simple, smart or stupid in order to fulfill some role, some image of what is thought to be acceptable. One is overly polite or solicitous—or quite the opposite. This is self-defeating because one then must live by a persona in which the self is not integrated and not real. A sense of self-acceptance is missing and this comes through in the way one relates to others. No one really knows who a person is including the person himself. Such an individual remains detached and cannot risk allowing defenses to come down. To access feelings means allowing others in, to trust—and to take the chance of getting hurt again. In such cases, the compulsion is to avoid, to evade, and to remove themselves from relationships that demand closeness. It may mean divorcing a spouse who needs more closeness; it may mean losing friends; it may mean losing the friendship of a child. For such individuals, it is preferable to be alone or even lonely than lower their guards. But it is not conscious. It is a compulsion to repeat, to repeat a retreat from potential hurts and injuries.

So we return—awareness and insight into one's self-sabotaging behavior and the origins of such behavior are first steps. But facing up to the self-defeating *result* of this behavior is also essential, as is the realization of one's view of himself as doomed to repeat. Insight is not only the recognition that troubling symptoms are causing problems, but that these *symptoms* have a *cause*. Things don't happen by chance and there are meanings to the symptoms. Symptoms can no longer be dismissed as some fluky aberration or some temporary quirk. There are reasons for these symptoms and occurrences. They do not occur over and over again for no reason. And it is a brave man or woman who dares to face up to these things.

We live in a society that tends to judge and criticize. We define thoughts and behavior in terms that logicians refer to as "the law of the excluded middle." Thinking and behavior are labeled as good or bad, right or wrong, black or white. This kind of thinking is the antithesis of a quest for meaning. It dismisses the fact that there may be an explanation for thoughts and behavior that is not fraught with judgment and criticism.

There are no sinners in therapy. It can be a very calming and freeing experience.

After recognition and awareness, comes the work of mourning[3]— mourning that injustices have been done, mourning that there was no one to listen when one needed to be heard, mourning the loss of opportunities for growth and change that have passed. Mourning and letting go is hard. It is really hard. Yet mourning is an essential ingredient in resolving self-sabotaging patterns. And many individuals caught in a compulsion to repeat are unable to mourn. Yet to move on, one must mourn, because mourning means recognizing—owning up to—the wasted and sabotaged relationships. It means owning up to one's own self-defeating behavior. It means owning up to what could have been, but never was. It means feeling the hurt and the pain of disappointment and neglect, of fear of loss at the price of one's sense of well-being. It means accepting the injustices of the past, the deprivations, disappointments, and neglects. It means giving up the fight for revenge, the fight for justice. It means seeing growth as letting go of the hurts—not viewing this as failure, but as movement toward the future. It means leaving behind the baggage of the past.

It does not mean that the past is to be denied, however. It must be owned as part of one's life's experiences. Ownership of the past allows one to move on to the future. It means realizing that one cannot expect a spouse, a boss, a child to make up to us in adulthood for what we did not receive in childhood.

It does not mean feeling sorry for ourselves or wallowing in self-pity. It does not mean martyring one's self. It does mean comprehending and owning up to the fact that the way we live our lives is not due to accident or happenstance. We may have to live with regrets. We *will* have to live with regrets. But it is important to see these regrets as an opportunity to move forward without this baggage of the past.

Reaching this point of realizing what we are doing, what we have been doing for many years, making the connections to our feelings, and getting in touch with those feelings, does not happen quickly or easily. It can be devastating to realize that one has spent a lifetime in such a way.

What else contributes to the resolution of repetitive cycles of self-sabotage? As long as we deny our role in our problems and fail to own up to our contribution, the cycle will continue. The tendency to deny and disavow our responsibility, to *disown* it, is widespread, and why not? It's hard to face the fact that I am the one who seeks abuse, that I am the one who undermines my relationships, that I am responsible for difficulties that I keep getting into with bosses, with marital partners, and with my children. This "owner-ship" means taking responsibility for what one has gotten oneself into.

Most often we know what we are getting into when we marry a certain person. Deep down, there may be doubts and uncertainties. We brush these aside and proceed with the marriage. Only later do we find that our doubts were well founded. We must accept responsibility for that decision.

We know that having children will change our lifestyle, will place restrictions on our freedoms, but we proceed to have children. And sometimes blame them when we cannot do what we want to do. The child did not ask to be born. The parent wanted the child. But that means assuming responsibility and avowing the willingness to assume accountability.

All of this "owning up" means facing sadness, uncovering pain, insults, and injustices.

Similarly, why would a person continue to identify with and try to please parents and friends who have their own agendas that involve misusing the person to meet their own needs? Why would parents visit their own unresolved problems onto their children? It means facing up to the fact that because my parents acted and treated me in a certain way does not mean I have license to do the same to those in my life now.

Cy's difficulty in committing to treatment, and in assuming re-sponsibility for missed sessions, and Jack's inability to face up to messing up his business are all indicative of problems in owning one's behavior.

And in marriage, ownership means avowing one's part in the unwritten contract. I married my spouse believing that he or she could and would be able to fulfill my needs, would be able to complement me in areas that I felt needed complementing. But these were my expectations and it was my judgment that I would be fulfilled in this marriage. Carlo believed that his efforts to return to school, to improve his place in the world, would be complemented by Mary. Mary expected that Carlo would be home every night and be involved in the family. These expectations were not fulfilled. Carlo had to own the fact that he broke the contract. He had been a carpenter with regular hours, coming home early every night to spend time with his wife and children. When he decided to further his education, there was a price to pay despite the fact that Mary agreed with what he was doing. Carlo chose to marry Mary and Mary chose to marry Carlo.

Yes, partners in marriage can change, can and do grow in different directions. One may want to maintain things as they are while the other may want to move on. But they owe it to themselves to recognize that they cannot blame the partner for everything. Seeking revenge for hurts and disappointments is a denial of responsibility for getting into and staying in a relationship that is filled with problems. Sometimes, the tendency is to collect injustices, to stew over vengeful thoughts, to live with them and to use them as part of a power struggle to keep one in a dominant position and the other in a subservient position. This is the opposite of acting responsibly, based upon the recognition that one has alternatives and choices, that doing unto others as was done to me perpetuates problems. They can stay in the relationship and try to move on, or they can terminate the relationship. Whichever choice these individuals make, it is their choice to live with.

How then do we interrupt repetitions? Forcing ourselves to change our overt behavior does not do it. Providing intellectual explanations for our behavior does not do it. Being told that we should try different approaches, that we should end relationships, that we should stop relating to others the way we do, or that we should get divorced does not solve the underlying problem. Essential to change is engagement in and commitment to a relationship with a therapist who is able to serve as the depriving parent, who is able to become the recipient of old distortions and angry feelings, who is able to accept the hostile outbursts which have been repressed, who is able to encourage the emergence of memories long forgotten and the emotions that went with them. It means relating to someone who is trying to feel with you what you have felt and what you have been through, while at the same time demonstrating how you have sought revenge when you were hurt, how you pushed away when you wanted closeness, how you used all this in repetitive, self-defeating behavior. Therapy means working with someone who is able to underline and clarify the nature and the meaning of your actions. It means developing a relationship where one can say and feel without fear of reprimand or criticism. It means becoming involved in an authentic relationship in which one does not have to play roles or to be someone fake.

It does not mean that the analyst is always right in his or her interpretations. It does mean that he or she is trying to tune in, to be on the same wavelength with one. It does not mean that the analyst can fulfill frustrations or that all the wrongs of the past can be corrected. It does mean that the therapist is there to try to help break the cycle, to allow mourning to occur, to provide a safe enough relationship so that one can risk removing the protective barriers that have prevented one from feeling those long-repressed, frightening memories.

It means being able to accept oneself as a real human being with assets and liabilities, strengths and weaknesses. It means one must accept that one no longer needs to pursue grandiose goals, to aggrandize oneself at every turn. But it also means not seeing oneself as an impotent and downtrodden victim, either. It means accepting mortality and limitations.

It certainly does not mean that all problems are solved forever. It does mean being aware of one's role in the self-sabotaging patterns of one's life and doing something about it. It means being able to make choices and to stand by them. It also means recognizing that they may not work out as we might have wished.

For the analyst, it means being there constantly and consistently, not judgmentally. It means encouraging the process of growing up and growing away, paving the way for feeling and being accountable.

Intensive psychoanalytic therapy is the approach of choice at the present time to deal with self-sabotage. This requires a long-term commitment, frequent sessions which are essential to getting to core issues, dealing with well entrenched defenses and working them out. Intensive work of this type is not popular at the present time for many reasons as pointed out earlier. But it is a step in the direction of the kind of self-examination that is necessary to break such cycles and to help one to become self-determining, and whole, again. It is a necessary step in learning that life is filled with choices and that our choices need not be based upon repeating the same mistakes over and over again.

Are there ways short of intensive psychoanalytic therapy that individuals can employ to help break these repetitive bonds? There are several, and some of them work well, both independently, as well as along with the therapy. I am reminded of an image I had long ago:

Suppose that one morning, a letter arrives at your door. Along with the bills and circulars, this one stands out. The handwriting is somewhat familiar, though you are not sure where you have seen it before. It's in a nice, thick envelope. You take it to your desk and set it there. But you do not open it.

The following morning, a similar envelope arrives. Again, you set it on your desk. Again, it remains unopened.

Days and days go by. Each morning, a letter arrives and never do you open one. An unlikely scenario, right? But it is what happens with so many of us, because the letters are our dreams, an important message from us to us. Inside all of us resides a dreamer, a poet, a child. And night after night, that mischievous child tells us a story. He or she takes weird events of the day and mixes them all up with weird events of long ago.

A woman has a baby, the baby is just two weeks old, but he can walk. Instead of being amazed, the onlookers are complaining that it's much more fun to watch a baby crawl.

What's that all about? Only you, the dreamer, know, because it is your dream. You dreamed it. Why? Who is the mother? Who is the baby? And why is this winsome, darling child walking—and why are the adults complaining?

Now, perhaps every reader could put an interpretation on this dream. Perhaps every analyst could think up a dream analysis. But only the dreamer of this dream can really tell, sometimes with some help and prompting, what it is all about.

Dreams tell us what we know, and, sometimes, what we don't want to know. Dreams tell us what is going on inside. They are springboards for creativity. They are important letters from us to us. Dreams can tell us much about how we are living our lives, where we are caught up in our lives, where we are making mistakes. Dreams resurrect people from our past. Why? What do they mean today? The alert dreamer can help herself to find her way through things that are bedeviling her.

A fire is raging in an abandoned building. The fire company arrives, but all of the firemen have no teeth. The dreamer is on the ladder going up to the fire, but the hose won't reach...

What is the fire? Why do the firemen have no teeth? What does that mean? Why won't the hose reach? Fires are almost always a symbol of extreme emotion—fear, rage, something intense. What does the fire say to this particular dreamer?

If a dream repeats itself in some form, night after night, if that letter tells the same story each morning, then that dream is especially important for the dreamer to consider. Why is there fire night after night? Is there rage during the day? And who is the rage turned toward? It is a wise dreamer who will consider these things. It is a rather simple step one can take to tune into what is going on inside oneself.

It's a good idea to write down the dreams if one can. I don't mean waking up in the middle of the night with a tiny flashlight, etc. However, on awakening, when remembering the dream, it can be very helpful to write down what it is that one has dreamed. Use the present tense. Sometimes, on rereading the dream, a phrase will jump out at you—some phrase that you wrote down. What does it make you think of? What is the *feeling* that you have in the dream? Did you feel frightened, happy, lonely? Connect to the dream. What is it that the baby tells me? Why dream of a baby? What is my connection to all of this? Remember, it is your dream. You made it up and everyone in the dream represents a part of you. It's an important letter from you to you.

In addition to reading those dream letters, there are other things individuals can do to bring some small degree of insight and resolution to some of their repetitive situations. It has already been mentioned that during a therapy session, musings, meanderings, wayward thoughts all have meaning. In one's quiet, inner life, these same fleeting thoughts can also have meaning. All thoughts *do* have meaning, if one can just take the time to consider them.

In real life, you see an old friend crossing the street, coming toward you. He does not as yet see you. You haven't seen him in a while, and he is someone you should be happy to see. But you turn away. You don't feel like talking to him right then. Why? Is there a reality issue at work here? Do you really have a time issue—perhaps a pressing meeting—and you can't afford to be late? Or is it something else? Why did you turn away? You can rationalize—I just didn't feel like it. But later, perhaps in some quiet time, you might turn your attention to that matter. What was wrong? What were you feeling? Were you afraid? Annoyed? Does this person represent a part of your life you would rather forget? Why?

Perhaps you feel yourself becoming exceedingly anxious every time you get in a car lately. You haven't been in an automobile accident, don't know anyone who has been. But at every intersection, you find yourself anxious, driving more slowly, more carefully. Why are you afraid? What makes you tense and anxious? Is the fear of accidents a hint of something else? Are you afraid perhaps of something looming, something that has nothing at all to do with driving? Are you feeling exceedingly fragile these days? Why? What is looming in your unconscious?

It could be even that things are not worrisome at all. It could be that things are going so well in your life that you feel it just must change, must get worse. *Things can't be this good for me.* That tells you something important.

Perhaps for no apparent reason you have been feeling sad lately, a heavy feeling inside you. Even with spring coming (or the holidays, or a vacation) the world seems dark and bleak. Getting out of bed in the morning is hard work. You look in the mirror and you even look sad, tired, your eyes red-rimmed. Why? No reason. Yes, I miss my mom, but she's been dead for years now. When did she die? Oh, my yes, three years ago this week. That's why I am feeling this way. An anniversary. Yes, but why sad? I didn't even much like her! Is that it? Maybe I'm feeling not so much sad, but angry? And therefore guilty?

Such things are hard to admit, but they do open doors. And often the sadness lifts. At the very least, it gives one the opportunity to know why one feels the way one feels. That in itself is freeing, especially if this is a repetitive cycle.

In addition to tuning in to one's inner life of thoughts and fleeting emotions, it can be useful to start paying close attention to the way others in your life react to you. Do people tread carefully around you? Do you inspire fear? Or are others cheerful and carefree in your presence? Are your children wary around you? How about the individuals with whom you come in contact on a peripheral basis? These encounters can sometimes be even more telling than the ones that take place within the family. Do you find shopkeepers friendly and open? Do people smile at you, greet you with warmth when you come to the same shop each morning for your coffee? Or do they respond with reserve? And how about *your* responses to others? Do you find friends all over the place, even at that miserable airport kiosk? Do individuals respond to you? Or do they shy away? What is the message that you are sending out?

It can be valuable to take some minutes out of every day, a kind of mental health checkup. Make the time to sit quietly, preferably when there is no one else around, in a room by yourself. Think about the events of the day—or perhaps, don't think. Try to sit quietly and see what comes. Sometimes ideas pop up, connections get made. It can be a very creative time if you can allow yourself to not program it. And if, day after day, the same thoughts and events pop up, it may be that these are the very repetitive symptoms of a repetitive cycle in your own life. It can be the start of dealing with those repetitions.

Another most useful thing one can do is to keep a kind of running account of what is going on in one's inner life by writing about it. Here, I don't mean a diary as such. Rather, one can employ a journal where one simply writes. Rant and rave on the page. Create poetry. Write about the awful boss, foolish wife, mean-spirited kids. (*No one should ever, ever, ever see this notebook.*) Of course, you love your kids, but they make you insane. Write it down. Maybe the squabbles with wife and husband seem to be repeated again and again—the same theme. He never listens to me; he misinterprets everything I say; she gives me the cold shoulder; sex is nonexistent. He's so damn cheap, she's a spendthrift. Why did I marry my father? Why must he drink? What can I do about it? What can I do about *me*? I'm so irritable this morning, don't know why, my life stinks, am so mad at my mother, the sun is shining, when will winter end, where are the kids socks, Danny has soccer this afternoon, Paul is irritating the hell out of me....

Rereading these notes, seeing the same theme, same words, day after day, tells us something. It tells what is going on in our lives. It can tell what is going on in your inner life. In addition to telling you something, such a journal can get rid of the petty stuff. As odd as it may sound, writing about it helps one to move on past it. The petty stuff can get left behind. (Who cares about the socks?) The bigger stuff jumps out and calls for recognition and awareness. It can be a most liberating experience. And if one does feel inclined to move onto therapy, there is plenty of information already plumbed from your unconscious that will help move you quickly along in the psychotherapeutic sessions.

In addition to writing about it, reading can help. There are loads of self-help books on the market that do give some insights into what is going on inside one, and hints about how to help. Some of these books are quite good, others, obviously, not so good. But go into any bookstore and there will be a literal smorgasbord of books from which to choose. Many of these offer simplistic solutions that are of no help. But some can offer at least some thoughts for ways to change one's life, to look at the cycles of one's life.

By now, of course, the reader knows that it takes much more than awareness to change these repetitive patterns. Sometimes, however, the awareness gained by reading can move one forward to the next step. Sometimes, oftentimes, one is unaware of what one is doing, as has frequently been pointed out here. But reading about it, perhaps reading this very book that's in your hands, can lead one to consider the repetitive habits of one's own life, and begin to make the necessary changes.

After reading all this, thinking about all of this, suppose one decides to begin this process of psychotherapy. Will it necessarily be long and painful and expensive? Maybe yes, maybe not. Some repetitions can be dealt with in a much shorter time frame, especially if one has made oneself open to the process by self-evaluation. So how does one go about finding and choosing a therapist? That is not the subject of this book, but a short mention is in order. There are many Web sites, listings of men and women in the field who are licensed and degreed, who have the necessary qualifications and training in this field. One of the best ways is to get a referral from a colleague or your family physician. And then, do a bit of digging on your own. Read about this individual. Interview him or her. Have a first meeting and see if it feels right, comfortable, see if there is a chemistry there. Just as in other aspects of life, one has a good feel for one person and not for another. The same applies to choosing a therapist. Consider if you would feel more comfortable working with a man or a woman. But be careful here: Sometimes, you might want to work with a woman, because you don't like men. It might be a good idea then to consider working out those problems with a man as therapist. And, of course, the same might apply to the feeling about women.

Another practical thing to consider here is cost. Find out if the individual is on your health plan. There is little sense in getting started with an individual, feeling comfortable, and then finding that you can't continue because the visits are not covered. (But bear in mind that most health plans place limits on the length and frequency of treatment they will pay for.)

All of these are simple ways to begin, perhaps even necessary ways to begin. But if one is truly intent on breaking the vicious repetitive cycle, one must begin. Tune into your inner life. Tune into your outer world. Consider all the places where you find yourself in the same bind again and again.

Is it scary to begin? Yes. Is it necessary in order to break the cycle? Yes.

It means ultimately, in spite of all the peripheral things mentioned above, entering therapy, beginning a journey with a professional "someone" who is able to help, to point out and clarify the meaning of your actions. It means developing a relationship where you can express what you really feel, say what you really mean, without fear, without judgment. It means becoming involved in an authentic relationship in which you do not have to play roles or to be someone fake.

There are no sinners in therapy.

And the journey is always worth it. It can and does change lives. And the journey itself can even be music.

References

INTRODUCTION

1. Freud, S. (1955). Beyond the pleasure principle. In J. Strachey (Ed. & Trans.) *Standard Edition of the Complete Works of Sigmund Freud.* Vol. XVIII, pp.7–64. London: Hogarth Press. (original 1920).

CHAPTER 1: REPETITION OF EARLY IDENTIFICATIONS: CONFORMITY VS. AUTONOMY

1. S. Rosner (1974), *The Marriage Gap.* New York: David McKay Co., Inc.

CHAPTER 2: REPETITIONS IN MARRIAGE: UNWRITTEN CONTRACTS AND COMPLEMENTARY REPETITIONS

1. S. Freud (1958), "Further recommendations on technique." In J. Strachey (ed. and trans.), *Standard Edition of the Complete Works of Sigmund Freud*, Vol. XII, p. 148. London: Hogarth Press (original 1914).

CHAPTER 3: REPETITIONS IN CHILD REARING

1. S. Rosner and E.M. Smolen (1963), "Observations on the use of a single therapist in child guidance clinics." *Journal of the American Academy Child Psychiatry*, 2(2): 345–356.

2. A.M. Johnson (1949), "Sanctions for superego lacunae of adolescents." In K. Eissler (ed.), *Searchlights on Delinquency*. New York: International Universities Press.

3. J.S. Wallerstein and J.M. Lewis (2004), "The unexpected legacy of divorce: Report of a 25-year study." *Psychoanalytic Psychology*, 21(3): 353–370.

CHAPTER 4: PENITENTIAL REPETITIONS: REPETITIONS OF RESCUE AND REPENTANCE

1. N. Friday (1977), *My Mother Myself*. New York: Dell Publishing.

CHAPTER 5. REPETITIONS ON THE JOB

1. S. Freud (1953), "The interpretation of dreams." In Strachey (ed. and trans.), *Standard Edition of the Complete Works of Sigmund Freud*, Vols. IV and V. London: Hogarth Press (original 1900–1901).

CHAPTER 6: REPETITIONS IN THE ADDICTIONS

1. S. Freud (1964), "Analysis terminable and interminable." In J. Strachey (ed. and trans.), *Standard Edition of the Complete Works of Sigmund Freud*, Vol. XXIII, pp. 209–253. London: Hogarth Press (original 1937).

2. P. Donovan (Oct. 19, 2000), *University of Buffalo Reporter*, Dopamine addiction, linked. 22(9).

3. J.D. Salamone, S. Mingote, and S.M. Weber (Jan. 21, 2003), "Nucleus accumbens dopamine and the regulation of effort in food-seeking behavior: Implications for studies of natural motivation, psychiatry, and drug abuse." *Journal of Pharmacology and Experimental Therapeutics*, 305(1): 1–8.

4. P. Carnes (1992), *Don't Call It Love: Recovery from Sexual Addiction*. New York: Bantam Books.

CHAPTER 7: THE REPETITION COMPULSION

1. S. Rosner (2000), "On the place of involuntary restructuring in change." *Psychotherapy*, 37(2): 124–133.

CHAPTER 8: RECOGNIZING AND RESOLVING SELF-SABOTAGING REPETITIONS

1. G.A. Bonanno (Jan. 2004), "Loss, trauma, and human resilience." *American Psychologist*, 59(1): 20–28..

2. D.W. Winnicott (1958), *Collected Papers: Through Pediatrics to Psychoanalysis*. London: Tavistock Publications.

3. P. Shabad (1993), "Repetition and incomplete mourning: The intergenerational transmission of traumatic themes." *Psychoanalytic Psychology*, 10(1): 61–175.

Bibliography

Carnes, P. (1992). *Don't Call It Love: Recovery from Sexual Addiction.* New York: Bantam Books.

Fenichel, O. (1951). *The Collected Papers of Otto Fenichel.* New York: W.W. Norton.

Fogel, G.I. (1991). *The Work of Hans Loewald.* Northvale, NJ: Jason Aronson, Inc.

Freud. S. (1958). *The Standard Edition of the Complete Works of Sigmund Freud*, 24 vols., translated by J. Strachey. London: Hogarth Press.

Friday, N. (1977). *My Mother Myself.* New York: Dell Publishing.

Javier, R.A. (2002). Review of *Trauma, Repetition, and Affect Regulation: The Work of Paul Russell*, J.G. Teicholz and D. Kriegman (eds.), New York: Other Press, in *Psychoanalytic Psychology*, 19(2): 409–415.

Johnson, A.M. (1949). "Sanctions for superego lacunae of adolescents." In *Searchlight on Delinquency*, K. Eissler (ed.), pp. 225–245. New York: International Universities Press.

Kampshaefer, G.M. (Chair/Moderator) (2005). Panel: Psychoanalytic work with self-defeating and self-punitive manifest content. Presented Div. of Psychoanalysis (39). American Psychological Association.

Luepnitz, D.A. (2003). *Schopenhauer's Porcupines: Intimacy and Its Dilemmas.* New York: Basic Books.

Marcus, J. A survivor's tale, Primo Levi article in *Amazon.com.*

Reik, T. (1941). *Masochism in Modern Man.* New York: Ferrar, Straus & Co.

Rosner, S. (2000). "On the place of involuntary restructuring in change." *Psychotherapy*, 37(2): 124–133.

Rosner, S. and Hobe, L. (1974). *The Marriage Gap*. New York: David McKay.

Rosner, S. and Smolen, E.M. (1963). "Observations on the use of a single therapist in child guidance clinics." *Journal of American Academy of Child Psychiatry*, 2(2): 345–356.

Sahbad, P. (1993). "Repetition and incomplete mourning: The intergeneration transmission of traumatic themes." *Psychoanalytic Psychology*, 10(1): 61–75.

Stern. S. (2002). "Identification, repetition, and psychological growth: An expansion of relational theory." *Psychoanalytic Psychology*, 19(4): 722–738.

Wallerstein, J.S. and Lewis, J.M. (2004). "The unexpected legacy of divorce: Report of a 25-year study." *Psychoanalytic Psychology*, 21(3): 353–370.

Winnicott, D.W. (1958). *Collected Papers: Through Pediatrics to Psychoanalysis*. London: Tavistock Publications.

Winnicott, D.W. (1965). "Ego distortion in terms of true and false self." In *The Maturational Process and the Facilitating Environment*, pp. 140–152. New York: International Universities Press (original work published 1960).

Index

About the Author

STANLEY ROSNER, Ph.D, is a Clinical Psychologist who has been in private practice for 40 years. He is a member of the Allied Professional Staff at the Norwalk Hospital Department of Psychiatry. He is also a Fellow of the American Psychological Association, the National Academy of Neuropsychologists, the Society for Personality Assessment, and the Connecticut Psychological Association. He has served as President of the Connecticut Psychological Association and President of the Connecticut Society of Psychoanalytic Psychologists.

PATRICIA HERMES is a Connecticut-based author whose work includes 40 novels for young readers. Her awards for her books include the Smithsonian Notable Book, the C.S. Lewis Honor Book, the California Young Reader Medal and the New York Library Best Book for the Teen Years Award.